Photo Elliott & Fry.]

Colonel C. E. DUFF, C.B.,
Commanding 8th Hussars.

Photo Dickinson.]

Lieut.-Colonel P. L. CLOWES, C.B.,
Late Commanding 8th Hussars.

8TH (KING'S ROYAL IRISH) HUSSARS.

DIARY

OF THE

SOUTH AFRICAN WAR,

1900—1902.

BY

J. W. MORTON,

SQUADRON SERGEANT-MAJOR,

Orderly-room Sergeant, 8th (King's Royal Irish) Hussars.

ALDERSHOT:
GALE & POLDEN, LTD., WELLINGTON WORKS.

1905.

8,828-j.

PREFACE.

This Diary is written from notes which were made daily when acting as signalling sergeant to Lieutenant-Colonel P. L. Clowes, C.B., who commanded the 8th Hussars during the war until October, 1901, and afterwards from notes when orderly-room sergeant. Major J. A. Henderson has kindly given permission for his Diary of C Squadron, when detached, to be published, and Major F. W. Mussenden has kindly supplied the Diary of B Squadron, when with Colonel Pulteney's Column.

J. W. MORTON, S.-S.-M.
(*O.R.S.*) *8th Hussars.*

ALDERSHOT,
23rd May, 1905.

NOTE.

As, during the War, it was impossible to always obtain an absolutely correct record of the Regimental number, rank, and name of all drafts and attached non-commissioned officers and men, I shall be obliged if, for the purposes of Regimental Records, any omissions or errors in the Christian names, Regimental numbers, etc., recorded in the following pages be notified to the Adjutant, 8th Hussars.

       C. E. DUFF, COLONEL,
          Commanding 8th Hussars.

ALDERSHOT,
23rd May, 1905.

INTRODUCTION.

The following is reproduced from the columns of the "Dublin Daily Express," dated 1st March, 1905, by kind permission of the Editor:—

SOME FACTS ABOUT THE 8TH KING'S ROYAL IRISH HUSSARS.

On the 28th January, 1693, an order was issued by King William III. commissioning Colonel Henry Conyngham (an ancestor of the present Lord Conyngham) to raise a regiment of dragoons in Ireland. The raising of the regiment was to be completed by March 20th, 1693, and the troops were ordered to rendezvous at Kilkenny and Clonmel. The corps thus formed now bears the title of the "8th King's Royal Irish Hussars." Conyngham's Dragoons remained in Ireland until the autumn of 1704, when they were ordered to embark for Portugal, in order to form part of the British force engaged in the war of the Spanish Succession. The regiment landed at Lisbon in November, 1704, but it did not strike its maiden blow until the 26th of January, 1706. On that day it formed part of a small force of 800 British and 400 Dutch troops, the whole commanded by its own Colonel, Conyngham, who were endeavouring to check the French advance upon Barcelona. The French force of 4,500 men, under D'Asfeld, attacked the allies at San Estevan de Litera. After a fierce combat, lasting seven hours, the French were beaten off with a loss of 400 killed and wounded. The allies lost 150 men, but their principal loss was in their gallant commander, Conyngham, who was mortally wounded and died two days afterwards. This action was pronounced by a writer of the period to be "as warm and glorious for the small body of men that were engaged as any that has happened this war." Colonel Conyngham was succeeded in the command of the regiment by Colonel Killigrew, and under the latter officer the corps served through the various phases of the campaign until the disastrous battle of Almanza, in which it lost two officers and over 20 men killed, one of the former being Killigrew, who fell whilst charging at the head of his men. The first two Colonels of the regiment were thus killed in action. Under Colonel Pepper, who was the next Colonel, the regiment greatly distinguished itself at the battles of Almenara and Saragossa. It is said that at the former battle a body of Spanish Horse were very roughly handled by Pepper's Dragoons, who tore the belts from the Spaniards' shoulders. In any case, the regiment was given leave to wear their belts over their shoulders, instead of round their waist like other Dragoons, and were known for many years as the "Cross-belt Dragoons." Pepper's Dragoons returned to Ireland in 1713, were disbanded for about sixteen months, in 1714-1715, and led an uneventful career in country quarters in Ireland and England until the year 1745, when, as "St. George's Cross-belt Dragoons," they assisted to defeat Charles Edward, the Young Pretender. In 1751 the regiment was numbered the 8th Dragoons. It then wore a scarlet uniform lined with yellow, and three-cornered cocked hats. In 1755 Lieutenant-General Richard St. George, the Colonel of the regiment, and, like Colonels Conyngham and Pepper, a distinguished Irishman, died in Dublin. In 1775 the regiment was designated the 8th Light Dragoons, and in 1777 was given the title of King's Royal Irish Regiment of Light Dragoons, and at the same time was granted the badge of the Harp and Crown, and the motto "Pristinæ Virtutis Memores." In 1794 the 8th were once more sent on active service, being ordered to join the Duke of York's army in the Netherlands. They landed at Ostend on the 1st of May, and very soon succeeded in distinguishing themselves, for on the 18th of that month the Royal Irish were sent forward to clear the village of Bouslieke (or Rousbeck), which was occupied by the enemy, who were in strong force, and who had planted a battery of guns in the churchyard so as to command the main street of the village. One squadron of the 8th charged up the main street, completely routing the French infantry posted to defend it, but suffering severely from the fire directed from the adjoining houses, and also from the fire of the battery in the churchyard. The gunners in charge of the latter, thinking themselves quite secure, remained at their post, but the Royal Irish, continuing their gallant charge, leaped the churchyard wall and captured the guns. "The spirited and distinguished gallantry" of the 8th on this occasion formed the subject of a general order, in which Lieutenant-Colonel Hart and his men were accorded the highest honour. On this hard fought day the 8th had no less than two officers and 95 men killed. The Royal Irish participated in the remainder of the campaign, earning praise for their conduct at the actions of Landmark, where they carried the bridge; Rouselaer, Kootmarke, Alost, and Boxtel, besides many minor affairs. The regiment returned to England at the end of 1797, but was less than a year at home, for in August, 1798, it embarked for the Cape of Good Hope, where it remained until 1802, with the exception of one troop, which was detached for service in Egypt. The 8th arrived in India in 1803, and formed part of the army which was concentrated at Muttra under General Lake. The regiment was then entirely mounted on white horses, and was commanded by Colonel Thomas Pakenham Vandeleur. Its first experience of Indian warfare was gained at the siege of Agra, but this was followed up by the cavalry action near Delhi, and shortly afterwards the regiment earned undying laurels by its brilliant charges at the battle of Leswarree. In this last battle Colonel Vandeleur and two other officers and sixteen men were killed. The regiment continued throughout the campaign, and took a distinguished part in the actions of Furruckabad, Dieg, Bhurtpore, and Afzulghur. At Afzulghur a squadron under Captain Deare succeeded, by a gallant charge, in rescuing a battery of artillery which had been cut off by the enemy. In 1808 the 8th were commanded by another distinguished Irishman, Lieutenant-Colonel Robert Rollo Gillespie, whose affection for the regiment remained undiminished till the day of his death. In 1812 one squadron took part in the operations against the fortress of Callinger; and in 1814, under Lieutenant-Colonel Westenra, the 8th formed a portion of the force engaged in the Nepaulese campaign, under the command of their former Colonel, Major-General Gillespie. In this latter capacity they were present at the assault upon Kalunga. Kalunga was a fort situated at the top of an almost inaccessible hill. General Gillespie directed its attack by a force of British infantry, but the assailants were driven back. He then formed up a dismounted squadron of the Royal Irish, and with the words, "Charge, boys, for the honour of the County Down," he placed himself at their head, and led the assault. The charge penetrated as far as the inner gate of the fort, but there Gillespie fell, the attack was unsupported, and the 8th were compelled to retire. Many gallant acts on the part of the 8th were recorded during this action. They lost, out of 100 men, one officer and three men killed, and four officers and 54 men wounded. General Gillespie's memory was honoured by a monument in St. Paul's Cathedral, and by an obelisk at his birthplace, Comber, Co. Down. After taking part in the siege of Hattrass in 1817, the regiment saw no further active service in India, and it returned to England in 1822. The conduct of the regiment during its twenty years' service in India had been so distinguished as to form the subject of a general order from the Governor-General on its departure from that country, and in 1825 this fact was further emphasised by an order directing the 8th to bear the word "Hindoostan,"

INTRODUCTION

as well as " Leswarree," on its standard and appointments. On the return of the regiment to England in 1823 it was equipped as a regiment of Hussars. It then remained in various country quarters in Ireland and England until the outbreak of the Crimean War, when it joined the expeditionary force to the East. In April, 1854, the 8th Hussars embarked for the Crimea, where they were destined to earn fame which will last for ever. They were present at the battle of the Alma, and on the 25th October, 1854, were the representatives of Ireland in the memorable charge of the Light Brigade. The 8th were the right supporting regiment, and, according to Kinglake, the great historian of the campaign, their advance down the fatal valley was executed with as much precision and accuracy as if they had been on parade, notwithstanding the additional difficulties and obstructions they met with in the shape of wounded and loose horses by which they were impeded, while being exposed equally with the first line to the heavy Russian fire. When the 8th, under Colonel Shewell, arrived at the end of the valley, the first line was completely broken up, with the exception of a small body of 15 men of the 17th Lancers, who thereupon joined the still compact 8th, and perhaps then laid the foundation of the strong and traditional friendship which has for so many years existed between the two regiments. Colonel Shewell then saw that three squadrons of Jeropkine's Lancers had come down on his right rear, and were preparing to cut off his line of retreat. Without hesitation he put his small force, now reduced to one squadron, about, and charged the three Russian squadrons. The 8th completely overthrew the enemy, and put them to flight, and consequently, in the opinion of Kinglake, the survival of the remnant of the Light Brigade was due to the gallant and timely action of Colonel Shewell and the 8th Hussars. The losses sustained by the 8th in the charge of the Light Brigade were very heavy. Out of a total of 116 engaged they lost 22 killed, 23 wounded, and 7 prisoners.

Amongst the killed was Viscount Fitzgibbon, whose statue now stands in Limerick. After taking part in the Battle of Inkerman and the Siege of Sevastopol, the 8th returned home in 1856, but were shortly again under orders for active service, for in October, 1857, they embarked at Queenstown for India, where their services were required to assist in quelling the Mutiny. The 8th Hussars formed part of the Central India Field Force, under Sir Hugh Rose, and greatly distinguished themselves in the long and arduous campaign which followed their arrival in India. At Gwalior a squadron of the 8th executed a most brilliant and successful charge, whereby the rebels were completely defeated, and two of their guns captured. In 1864 the 8th Hussars returned to England, and remained at home until 1878, when they again embarked for India. They took part in the Afghan Campaign of 1879-80, and remained in India until 1889, when they returned home, being thus the first British regiment to complete three tours of service in India, in each of which they distinguished themselves on active service. That the 8th were sportsmen as well as soldiers was proved by their winning the Indian Polo Tournament in two consecutive years, 1886 and 1887, and also by the many sporting trophies and distinctions gained by them during the eleven years they spent in India. The 8th were represented by a squadron in the Jubilee procession, 1897, and also furnished the escort to the Duke of York on his arrival in Dublin in August, 1897. The 8th Hussars left the Curragh for South Africa on February 13th, 1900, and arrived at Cape Town on March 10th, 1900. The 8th and 14th Hussars and the 7th Dragoon Guards formed the Fourth Cavalry Brigade. Their first engagement took place near Thaba'nchu, and they subsequently took part, under General French, in the main advance from Bloemfontein to Pretoria, being present in the fighting round Johannesburg and at the battle of Diamond Hill. They were next employed in the eastern advance to Belfast and Barberton. In October,

INTRODUCTION

1900, they came under the command of one of their own officers, General B. T. Mahon, who had previously relieved Mafeking, and in November they joined the Second Cavalry Brigade, under General Broadwood, in the Rustenberg district. Early in 1901 they took part, under General French, in the long and arduous "trek" to Piet Retief, and eventually into Natal. The headquarters of the regiment then remained for some months at Volksrust, whilst the squadrons were attached to the columns of the various commanders, including Rimington, Nixon, Pulteney, and Blomfield, and took part in the operations which were conducted by them, chiefly in the Eastern Orange River Colony and Transvaal, and in Natal and Zululand. In 1902 the regiment was concentrated under its own commander, Colonel Duff, and took part in most of the "drives" which were the closing feature of the campaign. The 8th remained in South Africa after peace was declared, and were stationed in Pretoria. They left Capetown on October 28th, 1903, and on November 19th, 1903, arrived at Aldershot, where they are now quartered. Few regiments have had a more distinguished fighting career than the Royal Irish Hussars, and no corps has borne a more important share in the great work of establishing our Indian Empire. The close connection of the regiment with Ireland has always been maintained, and such names as Conyngham, Pepper, St. George, Vandeleur, Gillespie, Westenra, and many others, prove that the 8th have always been Irish, not only in name, but in actual fact, and at the present time Major-General Mussenden, who took part in the charge of the Light Brigade as a cornet in the 8th, and who comes from the Co. Down, is Colonel of the Regiment.

8th (KING'S ROYAL IRISH) HUSSARS.

DIARY

OF THE

SOUTH AFRICAN WAR.

On Tuesday, the 26th December, 1899, orders were received at the Curragh Camp for the 8th Hussars to mobilize, and all the Reservists of the regiment, together with 50 Reservists of the 15th Hussars, were ordered to re-join the colours between the 28th December, 1899, and the 2nd January, 1900. The Reservists answered the call well, and, with only two exceptions, the 155 Reservists reported themselves at headquarters on the morning of the 3rd January, 1900, the greater part arriving on the last day.

The medical inspection was highly satisfactory, especially of the 8th Hussars, only a very small percentage being rejected by the medical officer.

On the 13th January, 1900, 139 more Reservists of the 15th Hussars were ordered to re-join the colours between the 18th and 22nd January, and their response was almost as satisfactory as that of the first portion, only four being absent, and of those one joined later.

Twenty-nine, however, were rejected by the medical officer.

The horses of the regiment had been infected with catarrhal fever, and this unfortunate circumstance had retarded the departure of the 8th Hussars for South Africa, much to the disappointment of Colonel P. L. Clowes and all ranks.

However, by careful supervision and strict isolation of the infected horses, this disease was at last stamped out, and on the 27th January, 1900, the Director-General of the Army Veterinary Department (Colonel Duck) paid an official visit to the Curragh and pronounced " A," " B," " C," and " Reserve " Squadrons free of all infection.

As, however, there were not sufficient horses fit for active service at the Curragh to make up the three squadrons and headquarters to the full war establishment laid down for the 4th Cavalry Brigade, to which the 8th Hussars had been appointed, " B " Squadron were ordered to proceed to Aldershot, dismounted, and accordingly, on Tuesday evening, the 30th January, Captain Thoyts, Captain Greathed (who had re-joined the regiment from the Militia), Lieutenants Mort and Threlfall, and 154 non-commissioned officers and men left the Curragh for Aldershot, where horses were provided for them by the Remount Department.

The remaining Squadrons, " A " and " C," were at once given their full complement of horses and brought up to full war strength with the horses left by " B " Squadron.

After considerable hesitation on the part of the War Office authorities and considerable uncertainty as to whether the 4th Cavalry Brigade would be wanted for South Africa or not, news was received on the 5th of February that Lord Roberts had cabled for the 4th Cavalry Brigade, composed of 7th Dragoon Guards, 8th Hussars, and 17th Lancers, and the next day an official intimation was received for the regiment to hold itself in readiness for immediate embarkation.

At first the War Office authorities decided that the headquarters and two squadrons should proceed to

SOUTH AFRICAN WAR

Aldershot, pick up "B" Squadron, and embark from an English port, but on representation of the prevalence of influenza at Dublin and among the horses at Aldershot, this plan was abandoned and the order given to proceed to Queenstown and embark on board s.s. "Norseman," of the Dominion Line.

HEADQUARTERS.

Headquarters, "A" and "C" Squadrons, were composed as under:—

Lieut.-Colonel P. L. Clowes, Commanding Regiment.
Major D. E. Wood, Second-in-Command.
Captain C. H. Campbell, Adjutant.
Second-Lieut. C. J. M. Lomer, Transport Officer.
Lieutenant and Quartermaster L. C. Page.
Major J. M. Irwin, R.A.M. Corps.
Civil Veterinary Surgeon J. Masheter.
1 Warrant Officer.
43 Non-commissioned Officers and Men.
9 Chargers and 21 Troop Horses.

"A" SQUADRON.

Major C. E. Duff.
Lieutenant E. A. S. O'Brien.
Lieutenant R. Lambert.
Second-Lieutenant Sir C. B. Lowther, Bart.
188 Non-commissioned Officers and Men.
6 Chargers and 147 Troop Horses.

"C" SQUADRON.

Major and Brevet Lieut.-Colonel B. T. Mahon.
Captain I. W. Burns Lindow.
Lieutenants F. H. Wylan and J. Van der Byl.
204 Non-commissioned Officers and Men.
6 Chargers and 146 Troop Horses.

The above left the Curragh Siding in three trains on the morning of the 13th February, at 4.0 a.m., 5.0 a.m., and 7.45 a.m., for Queenstown.

The weather was very severe. A deep snow lay on the ground, and a cold wind and a sharp frost made matters most unpleasant. However, in spite of all difficulties, each train got away in good time.

Queenstown was reached at 1.30 p.m., the horses were put on board as rapidly as the tide allowed, and the s.s. "Norseman" sailed at 8.30 p.m., amid a scene of enthusiasm from loyal Irishmen on shore and the troops on board.

Colonel Clowes assumed command of all the troops on board, which, in addition to the 8th Hussars, consisted of drafts of the 7th Dragoon Guards with horses, 18th Hussars (in charge of remounts), Royal Artillery, 2nd Dragoons, 5th Lancers, 9th Lancers, 14th Hussars, 4th and 5th Dragoon Guards, and the Duke of Cornwall's Light Infantry, the grand total on board being 26 officers, 1,100 non-commissioned officers and men, and 432 horses.

News was received from Captain Thoyts at Aldershot that he had been given 144 horses, and would embark at Albert Docks, London, on Saturday, 17th February, on s.s. "Sicilian."

The full total of 8th Hussars embarking for active service in South Africa was as follows:—19 officers (including medical and veterinary officers), 586 warrant officers, non-commissioned officers, and men, 29 chargers, and 458 troop horses.

SOUTH AFRICAN WAR 5

"A" SQUADRON,
8TH (KING'S ROYAL IRISH) HUSSARS.

NOMINAL ROLL OF THE N.C.O'S. AND MEN WHO PROCEEDED TO SOUTH AFRICA IN FEBRUARY, 1900.

Regtl. No.	Rank and Name.	Regtl. No.	Rank and Name.
2500	S.-S.-M. Stretch, F.	3114	Pte. Buxton, T.
2861	S.-Q.-M.-S. Nelson, A.	3439	,, Byrne, J.
2390	S.-S.-F. Williams, W.	4036	,, Byrne, M.
2178	Sergt. Tyler, J. R.	4117	,, Callaghan, P.
3028	,, Rawley, D.	3580	,, Clarke, G.
3266	,, Page, J.	3367	,, Clarke, G.
2842	,, Leopold, A.	3634	,, Codling, H.
3631	,, McKee, S.	3210	,, Coles, A.
4535	,, McKay, D.	3484	,, Coleman, P.
3357	,, Porter, H.	4243	,, Cullen, W.
3782	,, Morton, J. W.	3322	,, Cotter, E.
3296	,, Heatherall, C.	4173	,, Daly, J.
3661	Lce.-Sergt. Lewis, C.	4161	,, Donlon, M.
3637	Corpl. Hanbury, C.	4163	,, De Courcy, P.
3326	,, Ebbage, E.	2976	,, Driscoll, M.
3382	,, Champion, R.	3472	,, Doran, M.
2980	,, Burt, F.	4573	,, Dray, H.
3258	,, Courcou, T.	3851	,, Erswell, C.
3870	,, Pitchforth, J.	3016	,, Eyke, G.
3988	,, Jones, J.	3106	,, Foster, M.
3087	,, Pye, T.	3612	,, Fay, P.
2680	,, Knight.	4298	,, Fox, H.
2879	,, Symonds, R.	4127	,, Frain, M.
3201	Corpl.-S.-S. Kenny, T.	3080	,, Furlong, F.
3568	,, ,, Freeman, W.	3384	,, Gracey, S.
3817	Lce.-Corpl. Hodgson, R.	4309	,, Gill, A.
4050	,, Simpson, J.	2569	,, Gillespie, P.
4040	,, Dunn, F.	2854	,, Godwin, M.
4017	,, Marshall, P.	2923	,, Gordon, G.
4536	,, Banks, A.	4798	,, Goldsmid, S.
4046	,, Hunter, F.	4271	,, Greenwood, H.
3479	Tptr. Dove, H.	4148	,, Gregan, C.
4538	,, Burger, J.	3103	,, Griggs, W.
3059	S.-Smith Owen, J.	4233	,, Greer, A.
3506	,, Gledhill, C.	4563	,, Grummett, H.
4289	Act.-S.-S. Poole, H.	3581	,, Hamilton, A.
3003	Pte. Abbott, E.	3927	,, Hands, W.
4176	,, Bell, W.	3849	,, Haydon, M.
4295	,, Blackburn, P.	3720	,, Heather, A.
3841	,, Brown, J.	4151	,, Hendrick, J.
3844	,, Bowes, G.	3591	,, Henry, K.
3296	,, Bowen, H.	4291	,, Holmes, T.
3242	,, Bright, C.	2500	,, Houlden, T.
4036	,, Burns, O.	4560	,, Holland, W.

"A" SQUADRON, NOMINAL ROLL—(*Continued*).

Regtl. No.	Rank and Name.	Regtl. No.	Rank and Name.
2756	Pte. Holloway, W.	4146	Pte. Pender, J.
4569	,, Holgate, R.	2795	,, Pratt, W.
2842	,, Horne, G.	4090	,, Quigley, T.
2838	,, Hurt, J.	3741	,, Ranger, H.
2892	,, Hussey, J.	3321	,, Reilly, L.
2540	,, Jacobs, W.	3243	,, Richardson, A.
4646	,, James, G.	4065	,, Riley, J.
3124	,, Jones, J.	3684	,, Rivers, J.
3111	,, Johns, G.	4221	,, Rogers, G.
3981	,, Jefford, W.	3074	,, Robinson, H.
2835	,, Jenkins, E.	3853	,, Rudd, A.
2761	,, Jenkins, J.	3026	,, Saunders, W.
2866	,, Jenkins, G.	2931	,, Sagar, D.
2646	,, Jupp, G.	4227	,, Saylor, T.
2274	,, Kavanagh, W.	3281	,, Selman, F.
4664	,, Jordon, J.	2846	,, Short, C.
3219	,, Keogh, G.	3014	,, Smith, G.
3486	,, Kenny, R.	2743	,, Smith, R.
3525	,, Kellighan, E.	3447	,, Smith, T.
4174	,, Keenan, J.	3152	,, Snead, T.
3120	,, Kenworthy, E.	3836	,, Snead, T.
2890	,, Kemp, J.	3874	,, Sparks, T.
2981	,, Kirby, S.	3536	,, Shannon, C.
2714	,, Langridge, F.	2874	,, Southcote, A.
4509	,, Lewis, A.	4727	,, Simmonds, W.
4141	,, Leech, S.	2942	,, Squires, G.
3334	,, Little, S.	3943	,, Trainor, J.
4140	,, Lumley, E.	3565	,, Tait, T.
4048	,, Lusby, J.	2804	,, Taylor, C.
3443	,, Malt, C.	3518	,, Thompson, J.
3044	,, Manners, J.	3799	,, Thompson, W.
2849	,, Mayes, W.	2910	,, Thompson, W.
4105	,, McCabe, J.	2979	,, Tilley, W.
4072	,, McCormack, J.	4193	,, Timlin, M.
3616	,, McConnon, J.	3995	,, Wallace, E.
4087	,, McDonagh, B.	2915	,, Waller, C.
3972	,, McGinty, J.	3079	,, Wale, H.
3427	,, McGovern, M.	4546	,, Waldron, H.
3743	,, Middleton, A.	2853	,, Walkden, E.
3414	,, Miles, W.	3065	,, Webley, C.
3216	,, Mitchell, R.	3131	,, Whiting, W.
4078	,, Mooney, W.	3002	,, Williams, J.
4123	,, Morris, W.	4047	,, Wilson, F.
4093	,, Moore, H.	4265	,, Winstanley, R.
4726	,, Maud, F.	3032	,, Wynn, J.
2984	,, Murphy, P.	3070	,, Winpenney, J.
3567	,, Murtagh, B.	2887	,, Wood, J.
3994	,, O'Neill, J.	2749	,, Wood, C.
2568	,, Palmer, H.	3081	,, Yarwood, W.
3428	,, Parmenter, H.	2971	,, Yeo, J.

SOUTH AFRICAN WAR 7

"B" SQUADRON,
8TH (KING'S ROYAL IRISH) HUSSARS.

NOMINAL ROLL OF N.C.O'S. AND MEN WHO PROCEEDED TO SOUTH AFRICA, IN FEBRUARY, 1900.

Regtl. No.	Rank and Name.	Regtl. No.	Rank and Name.
2360	S.-S.-M. Spain, S. J.	4053	Pte. Fullerton, G.
2742	S.-Q.-M.-S. Hadler, W. R.	4286	,, Gadd, C.
2486	S.-S.-F. Brockwell, A.	4181	,, Galletley, J.
3105	Sergt. Barrett, E.	3523	,, Gibbons, P.
3362	,, Maloney, G.	4555	,, Graham, H.
3632	,, Hughes, J.	4301	,, Green, J.
3465	,, Bucklee, T.	4111	,, Griffin, J.
2512	,, Ogle, J.	4574	,, Gorman, T.
3641	,, Moore, R.	3704	,, Hannigan, T.
3353	Lce.-Sergt. Scudder, C.	4228	,, Harvey, W.
3736	Corpl. Kershaw, E. J.	2901	,, Hillerby, A.
3808	,, Pitchforth, R.	3789	,, Hughes, W.
3809	,, Cooper, W.	4230	,, Johnson, J.
3647	,, James, T.	3564	,, Kelley, D.
3788	,, Fyfe, L.	4340	,, Kenney, L.
4034	,, Conroy, J.	4235	,, King, J.
3379	Corpl. S.-S. Legood, W.	4247	,, McCaffrey, W.
3798	Lce.-Corpl. Nicholls, J.	4168	,, Mack, C.
4015	,, Lambert, H.	3710	,, Main, W
3670	,, Cook, W.	4261	,, Mann, W.
4108	,, Hindes, T.	4066	,, Miskelley, J.
3900	,, Martin, J.	4060	,, Morgan, W.
3577	,, Keeble, A.	3717	,, Morris, A.
3312	Tptr. Morris, H.	3976	,, McGuire, L.
3797	,, Cruse, W.	4547	,, McKinley, J.
3719	Saddler Lewis, J.	3660	,, Murphy, P.
4559	Pte. Abbott, G.	4002	,, Murray, C.
4714	,, Balls, J.	3490	,, Noone, P.
3984	,, Billane, J.	3666	,, Overington, W.
4553	,, Brown, W.	4216	,, O'Malley, J.
4135	,, Byrnes, R.	4177	,, Parkinson, J.
3674	,, Cameron, J.	4327	,, Parkinson, S.
4561	,, Chapman, C.	4156	,, Parrott, E.
3959	,, Connisbee, E.	3524	,, Press, J.
3528	,, Cross, G.	3600	,, Read, W.
4091	,, Cummings, J.	4283	,, Reilly, P.
3975	,, Cunningham, G.	3728	,, Rich, J.
4567	,, Cook, C.	3584	,, Russell, W.
3699	,, Cox, A.	3980	,, Scott, A.
3967	,, Dunn, J.	3749	,, Shetton, J.
4225	,, Farrell, W.	3675	,, Smith, E.
3687	,, Flowerdew, W.	4571	,, Sulton, H.
4079	,, Freebairn, J.	3642	,, Southam, F.

"B" SQUADRON, NOMINAL ROLL—(Continued).

Regtl. No.	Rank and Name.	Regtl. No.	Rank and Name.
3224	Pte. Shreeves, R.	3257	Pte. Ward, W.
4570	,, Scoble, H.	3393	,, Laing, R.
4208	,, Spencer, J.	3108	,, Connor, J.
4018	,, Thompson, D.	3090	,, Cotton, C.
3961	,, Tierney, J.	3125	,, Jones, F.
3551	,, Whelan, E.	3141	,, Lewis, T.
4113	,, Wilson, D.	3112	,, Mander, B.
4324	,, Wilson, H.	3133	,, Nicholson, G.
4651	,, Wood, W.	2506	,, Smith, F.
3386	Sergt. Harvey, G.	3148	,, Strange, A.
3397	,, Jarvis, A.	3116	,, Stanford, W.
3359	Corpl. Rayfield, W.	2919	,, Allen, F.
3352	Pte. Blows, T.	3015	,, Ames, J.
3383	,, Brennan, D.	2949	,, Burns, J.
3381	,, Battrick, F.	3060	,, Clarke, C.
3435	,, Brien, F.	3151	,, Donn, H.
3388	,, Cousins, J.	2989	,, Davis, H.
3513	,, Conway, T.	2066	,, Farrant, H.
3477	,, Dagg, R.	2972	,, Fisher, C.
3672	,, Dickens, D.	3000	,, Freeman, H.
3376	,, Duggan, A.	2957	,, Highland, J.
3350	,, Flemming, J.	3009	,, Hughes, E.
3901	,, Johnson, J.	3013	,, Jackson, C.
3452	,, Lawson, W.	3042	,, Julian, C.
3383	,, Morgan, J.	2989	,, Laffraty, C.
3442	,, O'Donnell, J.	2947	,, Lambert, W.
3311	,, O'Brien, F.	2953	,, Mapley, R.
3303	,, Rohan, J.	2992	,, Murray, T.
3487	,, Ramsey, J.	3001	,, Mitchell, J.
3510	,, Robinson, T.	3180	,, Mason, A.
3912	,, Short, G.	3047	,, Parker, A.
3402	,, Studd, A.	3268	,, Pittis, G.

SOUTH AFRICAN WAR

"C" SQUADRON, 8TH (KING'S ROYAL IRISH) HUSSARS, AND REGIMENTAL HEADQUARTERS.

NOMINAL ROLL OF N.C.O's. AND MEN WHO PROCEEDED TO SOUTH AFRICA IN FEBRUARY, 1900.

Regtl. No.	Rank and Name.	Regtl. No.	Rank and Name.
2933	S.-S.-M. Burns, J.F.	4166	Pte. Ennis, J.
2837	S.-Q.-M.-S. Reisland, N.	3993	,, Enright, P.
4532	S.-S.-F. Kirby, W.	3223	,, Everett, G.
3297	Sergt. Appleton, C.P.	3505	,, Farrell, E.
2947	,, Wilkes, W. G.	3795	,, Farrell, J.
3214	,, Kemp, E.	3532	,, Flanagan, M.
4537	,, Arle, C.	4270	,, Fleming, P.
3560	,, Walsh, D.	4404	,, Fleming, J.
2295	,, Bellett, E.	4407	,, Flood, R.
3714	,, Parry, E.	3706	,, Foord, C.
3544	,, Dye, T.	4006	,, Fraser, J.
3629	Lce.-Sergt. Moloney, W.	3924	,, Gillard, F.
3807	Corpl. McKay, S.	4332	,, Grant, J.
4541	,, Loft, A.	3689	,, Harbutt, L.
3813	,, Hodgetts, W.	3821	,, Hart, L.
3371	,, Hickey, G.	4545	,, Hart, E.
3299	Corpl. S.-S. Leopold, S.	4311	,, Healy, W.
3880	Lce.-Corpl. Cooke, G.	4501	,, Hickey, E.
3823	,, Hogg, W.	4248	,, Houliston, H.
4016	,, Hutton, A.	3645	,, Hughes, W.
3747	,, Grainger, E.	4236	,, Hughes, F.
4054	,, Bulcock, F.	3264	,, Kay, S.
3726	,, Walker, T.	4098	,, Kennedy, H.
3316	Tptr. Proctor, E.	4223	,, Keane, M.
3822	,, Hollingsworth, P.	3652	,, Kernon, T.
2845	Saddr. Muldoon, M.	4151	,, Kiernan, W.
3705	Pte. Abear, G.	3734	,, Lee, G.
3556	,, Adams, A.	4615	,, Lyons, M.
3793	,, Blowes, J.	4076	,, Maguire, J.
3882	,, Born, H.	3671	,, Maher, P.
4318	,, Broughall, T.	3678	,, Marshall, N.
4551	,, Burton, B.	4150	,, McCarthy, T.
4069	,, Byrne, M.	4171	,, McEvoy, T.
4229	,, Byrne, M.	4013	,, McDonald, M.
3583	,, Carroll, M.	3096	,, McKay, G.
4290	,, Carroll, T.	4126	,, McKenna, T.
4109	,, Chesters, P.	4138	,, McKeon, P.
4552	,, Coles, H.	4192	,, Moggie, J.
3848	,, Connors, B.	4349	,, Mulhall, C.
4086	,, Daley, J.	3728	,, Mullett, A.
4572	,, Davies, V.	3535	,, Murphy, J.
4182	,, Dickson, J.	3574	,, O'Connor, C.
4648	,, Doolin, J.	4299	,, O'Connor, P.
4393	,, Dyer, J.	4226	,, Page, E.

DIARY OF THE

"C" SQUADRON, NOMINAL ROLL.—(*Continued.*)

Regtl. No.	Rank and Name.	Regtl. No.	Rank and Name.
4175	Pte. Patterson, W.	4663	Pte. Spencer, C.
3599	,, Peacock, L.	3902	,, Walsh, T.
3460	,, Ramsay, W.	3134	Corpl. Fitzpatrick, J. C.
4154	,, Reilly, T.	2855	,, Sales, F.
3263	,, Ridings, P.	2828	,, Young, E.
3540	,, Routledge, J.	3058	Pte. Adkin, J.
3605	,, Rouse, A.	2998	,, Burrows, J.
3469	,, Secrett, T.	3054	,, Butcher, J.
3633	,, Shaw, J.	2958	,, Cook, F.
4186	,, Shea, D.	2988	,, Fielding, S.
3576	,, Sugars, G.	2993	,, Hales, C.
4107	,, Tait, W.	2781	,, Hall, H.
4562	,, Thompson, W.	2909	,, Harding, H.
4110	,, Tubby, A.	2727	,, Hillier, T.
4179	,, Ward, G.	2864	,, Huddleston, H.
4084	,, Welch, F.	2786	,, Ibbett, G.
4038	,, Wheaton, T.	2590	,, Inglis, W.
3947	,, Whiting, A.	2711	,, Jacques, E.
3744	,, Wildman, W	2684	,, Jennings, W.
4554	,, Woodworth, J.	2595	,, Johnson, W.
3467	,, Metcalf, T.	2797	,, Jones, A.
3459	,, Ray, F.	2799	,, Keyes, C.
4267	,, Morgan, H.	2639	,, Manning, W.
4565	,, Redington, A.	2717	,, McManus, A.
4222	,, Watson, J.	2843	,, McHugh, J.
4082	,, Gaffney, P.	2737	,, Mexted, H.
3440	,, Fitzgerald, M.	2550	,, Newman, R.
3618	,, Donnolley, J.	2818	,, Palmer, T.
3753	Corpl. Saunders, W.	2773	,, Puttick, A.
3117	Pte. Anderton, R.	2615	,, Richardson, G.
3105	,, Horton, G.	2945	,, Rodford, A.
3110	,, Lewis, J.	2742	,, Seward, A.
3126	,, Paul, J.	2735	,, Stevens, H.
3135	,, Sheargold, R.	2820	,, Stokes, A.
3433	,, Corpl. Goulder, R.	3021	,, Smith, A.
3438	Pte. Ayres, T.	2978	,, Tilley, G.
3457	,, Brady, P.	2881	,, Thompson, C.
3515	,, Cierey, J.	2652	,, Turnbull, H.
3380	,, Everett, W.	2968	,, Underill, J.
3476	,, Firm, M.	2662	,, Walter, T.
3403	,, Green, A.	2800	,, Weymouth, A.
3624	,, Hayes, G.	2893	,, Whitton, W.
3372	,, Kenny, M.	2694	,, Wicks, G.
3481	,, Kirwan, J.	2929	,, Williams, R.
3293	,, Lilley, W.	2845	,, Hillier, F.
3377	,, Legood, J.	2647	,, Watkins, E.
3492	,, Lynch, M.	2757	,, Ward, G.
3205	,, Miles, F.	2908	Sergt. Reed, E.
3607	,, Overton, J.	2084	,, Wilson, B.
3483	,, Pluck, J.	3285	Corpl. Garrett, J.
3218	,, Smith, R.	2619	Pte. Jeffrey, W.

SOUTH AFRICAN WAR

"C" SQUADRON, NOMINAL ROLL.—(*Continued.*)

Regtl. No.	Rank and Name.	Regtl. No.	Rank and Name.
2896	Pte. Joslin, J.	3480	Tptr. King, F.
2771	„ Johnson, W.	2314	Pte. Brien, J.
2886	„ Knight, H.	3546	„ Butcher, J.
2540	„ Maisey, C.	4003	„ Casson, H.
2836	„ Nicholas, G.	3359	„ Chamberlain, —
2851	„ Over, L.	3588	„ Chote, A.
2744	„ Purchase, W.	4498	„ Connealley, M.
2812	„ Palmer, J.	3098	„ Coe, W.
2552	„ Regan, J.	3406	„ Cooper, E.
2668	„ Richardson, H.	4026	„ Flannery, J.
2576	„ Sheriff, F.	4310	„ Freeman, F.
2765	„ Stone, E.	3922	„ Geall, A.
2805	„ Sutton, H.	3364	„ Gilbert, W.
2865	„ Tonge, W.	4155	„ Greenstreet, W.
2916	„ Tudguy, J.	3132	„ Green, G.
3019	„ Terry, T.	3926	„ Grundy, S.
2682	„ Wilmott, E.	3369	„ Hayes, H.
1725	R.-S.-M. Mountford, W.	4308	„ Fairclough, —.
2203	F.-Q.-M.-S. Swarbrick, J.	3697	„ Hiorns, H.
2598	O.-R.-Q.-M.-S. Hampton, R.C.	4122	„ Howarth, J.
2327	Saddr.-Sergt. Burrell, R.	3832	„ Hutson, J.
705	Arm.-Sergt. Smallwood, —	3102	„ McKay, W.
2355	Sergt. Mellish, H.	4103	„ Payne, J.
3246	„ Joice, W.	3414	„ Reeves, J.
3748	S.(O.R.C.) Brand, C.W.	3328	„ Stacey, H.
3553	Lce.-Sergt. Griffiths, A.	3534	„ Sweeney, M.
2865	Corpl.-S.-T.-M. Prince, P	4011	„ Turner, T.
3775	Corpl. Marston, T.	3968	„ Walker, B.
3825	„ Rayfield, S.	3388	„ Wiley, W.
3262	Lce.-Corpl. Everett, W.	4097	„ Wymberry, D.
3669	„ Lusher, J.		

RESERVE SQUADRON.

A Reserve Squadron, strength 500 non-commissioned officers and men and 200 horses, was left behind at the Curragh on the regiment embarking for South Africa.

OFFICERS ON SPECIAL SERVICE.

1. Major and Brevet Lieut.-Colonel P. L. Le Gallais, on special service.
2. Captain J. A. Henderson, in command of Brabant's Horse.
3. Captain F. Mussenden, in command of a squadron of Brabant's Horse.
4. Captain H. F. Deare, attached to Remount Dept.
5. Lieutenant P. A. T. Jones, seconded for service in South Africa.
6. Lieutenant F. M. Jennings, attached to 10th Hussars.
7. Captain and Riding-Master E. G. Tomblings, specially asked for by Field-Marshal Lord Roberts for employment with Remount Department. Captain Tomblings sailed on board s.s. "Canada" en route to Cape Town on the 12th February, 1900.

13TH FEBRUARY, 1900.—There had been a heavy fall of snow on the 12th. That evening all were busy making preparations for our early morning move next day. We left the Curragh Siding to the accompaniment of strains from the band of the 21st Lancers, and arrived at Queenstown. The embarkation on board the Dominion liner s.s. "Norseman" proceeded rapidly, and at 8.30 p.m. we steamed out of Queenstown Harbour, amid a display of fireworks from the loyal inhabitants. Several bands played until we passed out into the darkness of the night.

14TH.—Sea fairly heavy. Many sick.

15TH.—Very cold, snow and sleet fell.

FEBRUARY, 1900.

16TH.—One horse died.
17TH.—Three horses died.
18TH.—Church service, conducted by Colonel Clowes on the main deck. We passed Madeira at 11.30 a.m. Sea very calm.
19TH AND 20TH.—Beautifully calm sea.
21ST.—One horse died.
22ND.—Arrived at St. Vincent at 8.0 p.m. Anchored at 11.0 p.m.
23RD.—Coaling. My first experience. Everyone and everywhere showed signs of coal dust. Most unpleasant. Crowds of natives endeavouring to sell fruit, etc.; this is hauled on board by ropes made fast and baskets attached.
St. Vincent is a strongly fortified town. The cliffs rise sheer from the water. Little or no vegetation to be seen. S.S. "Avoca" in Bay carrying wounded from Colenso home. Left at 4.0 p.m. Passed many islands during afternoon and evening.
24TH.—Sea calm. Two horses (including Major Duff's charger) died. I was inoculated for enteric. The process of inoculation (in the side) is simple and practically painless. The medical officer takes a piece of skin between his fingers and inserts the point of a small hypodermic syringe containing the fluid to be injected. The after effects are certainly not pleasant. Every bone in one's body seems to ache and a great thirst prevails. Many on board were inoculated and soon recovered from the effects. Two or three days are sufficient to lay up.
25TH.—Two more horses died.
26TH.—Crossed the Equator. Customary visit from Father Neptune.
27TH.—The boat was stopped to-day to allow the Reservists on board to have musketry practice. A boat was lowered and took out a floating target which was placed astern. Several sharks seen.
28TH.—One horse died. Boxing contests commenced.
1ST MARCH.—A stoker or trimmer of the ship's crew,

MARCH, 1900.

named Griffiths, died from pneumonia, and was buried. Colonel Clowes read the burial service.

2ND.—Through the kindness of the Company the troops were now provided with a cup of tea or coffee night and early morning. Cleaning of ship commenced. Bedding inspection.

3RD.—Water running short. Learn that if it becomes necessary to condense water, the ship is forced to run at one-third speed. Head winds.

4TH.—Usual church service. One horse died. Head winds.

5TH.—Shall not reach Capetown as soon as expected owing to head winds and the cross currents we are at present encountering. Do not now expect to reach Capetown before Thursday.

6TH.—Head winds.

7TH.—Head winds, rough sea.

8TH.—Same again to-day. Shall not get in. Foggy evening.

9TH.—Reveillé 4.0 a.m. At 7.0 a.m. we had not sighted land. Slowed down, and finally stopped at 7.30 a.m. Sighted other transports also waiting for fog to clear.

When at last we could see the celebrated Table Bay, it was evident that something unusual was taking place in the country in which we were about to land. Camps were dotted along the shores, large numbers of transports, all bearing their number largely written on the bows, were seen.

I had formed an idea of a harbour such as this, with its celebrated mountain overshadowing it, its sandy shores, its pretty adjacent town, Simon's Town, and many other interesting features, and I was agreeably surprised to find everything exceed my expectations.

If ever a regiment landed with a good heart and in the pink of condition, the 8th (King's Royal Irish) Hussars, *i.e.*, " A," " C," and " H.Q." Squadrons, did on the 10th, when we were heartily welcomed by a party of loyal

MARCH, 1900.

Colonial ladies, and given a cup of tea, a bag of grapes, and some biscuits.

There was a high wind blowing as we marched to Maitland Camp, about four miles distant, choked with dust, and more than glad to have arrived at our first camp.

11TH.—Our first experience of South African weather was not pleasant. Our camp was a sandy one; it was very windy, and very warm. A strong combination of these three made things most unpleasant. Most of us bought sand glasses. By good luck I bought a good pair, and very glad, too, that I did afterwards, for Captain Jennings, our signalling officer, who some months later was only recovering from a blow in the eye from a locust, lost the pair he was accustomed to wear, and was pleased to accept this same pair of mine.

In the evening I visited Capetown and had a walk round. Refreshments were very dear. Bottle Bass 2/6, ordinary beer 1/- per bottle, and others in proportion.

Major and Brevet Lieutenant-Colonel B. T. Mahon, D.S.O., left the regiment and proceeded to take over command of the Colonial Corps.

12TH.—Parade in marching order.

13TH.—Ordinary parade to help to get horses in condition.

15TH.—Ordinary routine.

16TH.—" B " Squadron arrived in camp. They had a breakdown coming over, and although they left before us, we beat them during the journey, so the poor " Special Service Squadron," as they were jokingly dubbed on leaving Ireland for Aldershot, was greatly disappointed. P.V.O. held an inspection, and was well pleased with the result.

17TH.—Church (open air) service conducted by the clergyman who is to accompany one of the brigades. It was a very impressive service.

19TH.—Captain H. F. Deare rejoined regiment from his employment on Remount Department.

MARCH, 1900.

20TH.—"C" Squadron and headquarters left to-day for Norvals Pont.

23RD.—Lieutenant Taylor, 19th Bengal Lancers, attached to the regiment.

20TH TO 26TH.—This week was spent in daily exercise getting the horses fit.

22ND.—Lieutenant P. A. T. Jones re-joined from special service.

27TH.—"A" and "B" Squadrons entrained at Capetown for Norvals Pont.

Our party had 1st class F.S. carriages and a grand ride up country. All along the line we ran across traces of the war, broken culverts and bridges that had been repaired, graves and dead horses were to be seen everywhere. We passed through Colesburg and Arundel. At Matjestfontein, in the distance, we saw General Wauchope's grave —a monument had been erected over it.

We arrived at Norvals Pont on the Orange River, detrained, and watered our horses there. The bridge over the river had been destroyed, but one was able to imagine what a splendid structure it must have been prior to its destruction. The Engineers had erected two pontoon bridges across near to the original bridge, one for rail and one for foot. These are said to be two of the largest or longest pontoon bridges ever built.

I must now turn back to "C" Squadron and headquarters. These arrived at Norvals Pont on the 22nd inst. and proceeded by march route to Bloemfontein on the 29th, bivouacking en route as follows:—

29TH.—Donkerspoort.
30TH.—Priors.
31ST.—Springfontein.
1ST APRIL.—Jagersfontein.
3RD.—Krugers.

On the 4th, Edenburg was reached, where, on arrival, orders were received to march at once to join General Gatacre's force. General Gatacre had retired before

APRIL, 1900.

squadron arrived before Reddersburgh, and squadron marched to Bethany and bivouacked.

5TH.—Kaffir River Bridge.

6TH.—Kaal Spruit.

8TH.—Bloem Spruit Camp.

9TH.—Donker Hoek Camp (about 6 miles N. of Bloemfontein). "A" and "B" Squadrons' journey from Norvals Pont was only marked by one incident. We were stopped at Kaffir River Bridge and ordered to place a guard in the baggage trucks as it was rumoured that the Boers intended to attack the train and destroy the line. Every precaution was taken, and full orders issued to each party of the course to be adopted in case of an attack. However, nothing happened, and we reached Bloemfontein at 4.30 a.m., 3rd April, 1900.

4TH.—We left in the afternoon for brigade camp, but lost our way, and camped in heavy rains and without anything to drink and nothing but a biscuit to eat (our first experience).

5TH.—We reached the brigade camp at Donker Hoek.

7TH—General French inspected the camp. The brigade now consisted of 7th Dragoon Guards and 8th Hussars.

9TH.—Captain F. W. Mussenden re-joined regimental headquarters from special service with Brabant's Horse.

Lieutenant P. A. T. Jones was to-day re-appointed adjutant on re-joining the regiment, after having been on special service in South Africa since November.

11TH.—Some Boers made their appearance, and the brigade turned out. The reconnoitring patrol, under Captain Burns Lindow, fired a few shots, and Boers retired.

13TH.—Lieutenant F. M. Jennings re-joined from 10th Hussars.

15TH.—Second-Lieutenant Sir C. B. Lowther joined from base at Bloemfontein.

c

April, 1900.

16TH.—Lieutenant Jennings appointed signalling officer to the 4th Brigade.

7TH TO 20TH.—We remained at Donker Hoek, about six miles from Bloemfontein. During this period the 4th Cavalry Brigade was formed, and consisted of 7th Dragoon Guards, 8th Hussars, 14th Hussars, and "O" Battery, Royal Horse Artillery. The fortnight's rest here was, I believe, really arranged to give the mounted troops that had been actively engaged round Thabanchu, Sannas Post, and Karee Siding, a much needed rest, and to enable suitable remounts to arrive.

The regiment spent the time in making every effort to take the field as complete in every detail as possible.

We had some bad weather, and our first experience of a really violent storm of thunder, lightning, hail and rain. It was bad enough in tents, but we had afterwards many worse experiences in the open. At Donker Hoek there was only one casualty—one man of the 7th Dragoon Guards killed on outpost duty by a Boer sniper.

21ST.—We moved to Springfield.

4th Cavalry Brigade, under the command of General Dickson.

22ND.—We moved out of bivouac and had our baptism of fire at Donkerspruit early in the day's operations. A heavy pom-pom fire was the first to greet us quite unexpectedly, "C" Squadron engaging a party of the enemy with rifle fire. For about half an hour we had a very lively time, but retired out of range with a loss of Trumpeter Cruse killed and Private Cox wounded, 3 horses killed and 3 wounded. To-day was the first experience I had of signalling on service and during the engagements. I was on the General's Staff during the Thabanchu operations, and found how valuable the heliograph was and what an important part it must play in all operations and engagements in any country like South Africa. General Pole Carew, who was in command of

SOUTH AFRICAN WAR

APRIL, 1900.

the operations to-day, directed them by this means, our first message reading:—

"G.O.C. 4th Cavalry Brigade. Am attacking Kranspruit Farm. Please protect my left flank and co-operate as far as possible. G.O.C. 18th Brigade."

No. 3977, Trumpeter Cruse was killed in action.
No. 3699, Private Cox wounded.

23RD.—Lieutenant Taylor, 19th Bengal Lancers, attached to regiment.
Marched at 7 a.m., joined 3rd Cavalry Brigade, and bivouacked at Tweegeluk.
No. 2972, Private E. Fisher, reported "missing"; afterwards re-joined.

24TH.—At sunrise I was sent out of camp to a small kopje, and, following instructions received, flashed my helio rapidly round a limited area, and received the following message for General Dickson from General French:—

"The 4th Cavalry Brigade will concentrate near the farm 4 miles N.W. of Leeuw Kop as early as possible. Communicate first and be careful to render any assistance to G.O.C. 18th Brigade before leaving."

To-day's fighting lasted from 6.0 a.m. until 4.0 p.m. Colonel Clowes was brigadier, and as the day's casualties in the Cavalry Division amounted to 1 officer and 7 men killed, and 30 officers and 23 men wounded, and 90 horses rendered hors de combat, we were glad of nightfall.

Regimental Casualties.—No. 4283, Private P. Reilly, severely wounded; No. 3350, Private J. Fleming, 3717, Saddler J. Louis, 3912, Private G. Short, all of "B" Squadron, slightly wounded; 1 horse killed and 1 wounded. Bivouacked at Grootfontein.

25TH.—Reveillé 4.0 a.m. Fixed up communication with outpost lamp by means of a blanket and a candle.

APRIL, 1900.

Our object to-day was to try to cut off Boers at De Wetsdorp. At 7.30 p.m. last night I transmitted the following message to General French from Sir Leslie Rundle, begins:—" Am 4 miles W. of Dewetsdorp. Enemy holding a strong line facing W. and S.W. 5 or 6 miles long, strongly entrenched, covering Dewetsdorp. They have 5 or 6 guns and their force is variously estimated at from 6 thousand. Please helio to me your opinion to-morrow." Ends.

There was a little firing on our flank—17th Lancers—but not much fighting.

To-day General Carew was ordered to hold his position until Wepener was relieved. The regiment bivouacked 1 mile N. of Dewetsdorp.

26TH.—Marched at 6.0 a.m. We were issued with two days' rations to-day, viz.: 5 biscuits and 1lb. of meat. Not much fighting.

27TH.—Marched at 7.0 a.m. " B " Squadron, under Captain Thoyts, came in contact with the Boers. No casualties, Sergeant Hughes, shot through the sole of the boot, having a narrow escape. Bivouacked 3 miles S. of Thabanchu, near Wildebeest-Spruit.

28TH.—A very busy day. To commence we worked on the right flank of the Boer position, and passing their flank under a fairly heavy shell fire, commenced working at the Boer rear, endeavouring to join the 1st Brigade, so as to cut off the Boer retreat. Advance patrols were sent to find Colonel Gordon's Brigade, but constantly reported by helio that no signs of them could be seen. General Dickson, Lieutenant Jennings, and Captain Taggart, brigade-major, and myself, with helio, were on a small kopje near a kraal. We were in communication with General French through General Hamilton. About noon we saw large numbers of Boers, who at one time had been hurrying away in rear, coming again across the plain. Our brigade had so weakened itself by the number of patrols sent out, that the General heliographed

APRIL, 1900.

for urgent reinforcements of mounted infantry from General Hamilton.

These eventually arrived, but too late to stop the Boers assuming the aggressive. Just before their arrival General Dickson helioed to General French: "Am compelled to retire."

The Boers entered the gap at the foot of the kopje as we came down the slope, but we just managed to get away in time.

So quickly had we to come down that glasses, maps, haversacks, and food, to say nothing of a fine turkey that had been bought by the General, were left for Johnny Boer, who also "borrowed" our regimental water cart and driver from the foot of the same kopje. We retired quietly on Thabanchu, reaching there quite late, Boers sniping at us in the dark. The blue spits of flame from the sides of the kopjes held by the Boers had a pretty effect in the fast coming darkness.

No. 3674, Private S. Cameron, wounded to-day near some Kaffir Kraals whilst on patrol.

No. 2684, Private W. Jennings, reported "missing"; since re-joined.

No. 4176, Private J. Bell, reported "missing," but subsequently re-joined.

29TH.—This morning the troops were permitted to rest until quite late, comparatively speaking. Boers sniped at us from long range as we watered at a spruit a short distance from our bivouac. After watering we retired under cover of a neighbouring hill and off-saddled, the horses being allowed to graze a short distance away. Suddenly, bang!—a Long Tom had opened fire on us. The horses were brought in and properly saddled, despite the continued attentions we received from this unwelcome visitor, and, after every man had saddled we rode quietly out of our bivouac and took shelter behind a long ridge close by. We were lucky to have no casualties except one horse killed, for the Boers had, one might say, a fixed

APRIL, 1900.

target to aim at for a quarter of an hour. Our convoy got away with the exception of the wagon containing the officers' mess food, utensils, and the officers' baggage, which was overturned and pitched into a donga. During our retirement, and just before reaching the donga mentioned, I saw a Boer shell fall in the centre of a small ring of infantrymen who were sitting down cooking their food, wounding two of them. About noon we were ordered out of camp to proceed along the De Wets Dorp Road to the assistance of Colonel Gordon, 1st Cavalry Brigade, who was supposed to be hard pressed on the Khabanyana River. We did not go far, however, before news was received that he had extricated himself, and we were ordered to camp—Taballi, $2\frac{1}{2}$ miles S.E. of Thabanchu. It was then quite late at night.

30TH.—Reveillé 5.30 a.m. Grazed in the morning, but about noon we were ordered out to assist a convoy. After saddling and standing to for a time we were ordered to off-saddle and then indulged in a quiet day.

1ST MAY.—Reveillé 5.30 a.m. The regiment and a composite regiment, consisting of a squadron from each of the 16th, 17th, and 9th Lancers, and "O" Battery, Royal Horse Artillery, the whole under command of Lieutenant-Colonel Clowes, 8th Hussars, turned out to assist General Ian Hamilton at Hout Nek, where he was hard pressed. Our object was evidently to get well to the Boer flank and threaten his rear. This was ably accomplished without casualty, despite a fairly warm Mauser fire for a short time. Whilst trotting along in extended order one could plainly see the little spits made in the sandy ground by the bullets as they dropped round about. These had not been noticed before owing to the ground over which we had previously worked being of a hard nature, and had not allowed of our seeing this effect. We chased the enemy well back towards Taba Mountain and took a number of prisoners. A Boer Commandant was found badly wounded under the crest of the hill where, a few hours before, Captain Towse, Gordon Highlanders, had been severely wounded, losing the sight of both eyes. It was 9 p.m. before the troops reached Taballi Camp, after a long but useful and interesting day's work, for which we were highly commended by General Hamilton.

No. 3822, Trumpeter Hollingsworth, missing.

No. 3684, Private J. Rivers, died of dysentery at Donker Hoek.

2ND.—Busy signalling in camp all day. The brigade was expecting to be called out as the enemy was seen in the vicinity of the outposts. Captain Miller, of the 14th Hussars, who was out with a patrol, was captured whilst scouring the country in front of the outposts.

Major Duff to-day made every non-commissioned officer and man a present of half a pound of hard tobacco —a most acceptable present, as our small stock had run out.

No. 3674, Private Cameron, wounded on outpost.

3RD.—Commenced our return journey to Bloemfontein, passing the celebrated Bushman's Kop, and bivouacking near the Waterworks—the scene of the Sannas Post disaster.

4TH.—Arrived at Donker Hoek.

5TH AND 6TH.—Remained at Donker Hoek, obtaining some necessary stores from Bloemfontein. Lieutenant G. M. Mort and Lieutenant and Quartermaster L. C. Page admitted to hospital.

7TH.—Left Donker Hoek Camp and commenced our march to Pretoria. We were all in the highest of spirits, and although we made a bad start by our convoy wandering astray and leaving us without rations on the first night, no one seemed to mind very much—excitement on this occasion perhaps helped to fill up one or two gaps. Bivouacked at Roodeheuval.

8TH.—Reveillé 4.30 a.m. Brigade orders said "March at 6.30," but no convoy, and, therefore, no food, having

MAY, 1900.

arrived, we were allowed to wait a little time in the hope that both man and horse would be fully provisioned before commencing the day's march. It did not arrive, so we marched and overtook it at Brandfort, halting there till man and beast were refreshed. An engagement had been fought here some days previously, and the town was depleted of food. There was, in fact, nothing one could purchase in the town but sugar, and that was 1s. 3d. per pound. Camped at Vet River.

9TH.—Reveillé 3.45 a.m. To-day's was a very long day's march. No signs of the enemy were seen. Bivouacked at Kalkoenkranz.

10TH.—Reveillé early, and a very cold morning. The 1st Cavalry Brigade were in advance of ours, and we had to march rapidly in an endeavour to catch up to them. We passed several diamond mines at Posen. On our right, and slightly to our front, we saw the balloon of Lord Roberts' force making observations.

On reaching the 1st Cavalry Brigade we found them having a very warm time of it from Mauser, pom-pom, and big gun fire. We passed to their flank and immediately received the attention of the Boer Artillery. The enemy did not, however, permit us to get far round their flank before making an attempt to stop us. About 200 mounted Boers came down from a kopje which they held, and, riding at open files, advanced to within about 1,000 yards of the brigade, when they halted, dismounted, and opened fire. The regiment was ordered to charge. What a " charge " it was. The horses had not been fed or watered that morning, we had come a good distance at a good pace, and, equipped in full marching order, carrying rations for horse and man, could barely raise a decent gallop. With cool effrontery, the Boers mounted, and, riding back some distance, dismounted and fired several rounds each, and once more repeated this performance. Eventually our best mounted reached a few of their stragglers, who paid the penalty of their temerity.

MAY, 1900.

The order was then given to our troops to return, and we did so with two prisoners. The enemy turned on us again, and, assisted by a gun from the hill, endeavoured to hasten our return. Our troops trotted back in a leisurely manner with one casualty in the advance and retirement—Private Coles—slightly wounded in the side. However, we had accomplished our General's object, and had accounted for two Boers killed and half-a-dozen wounded. In conversation with one of the prisoners afterwards I asked him to account for our small casualty list, taking into consideration the reputed clever marksmanship of the Boers in bringing down buck on the move. He excused his comrades' bad shooting, remarking " It is a far different thing to fire at a man riding at you with a drawn sword, even if he be some distance away, than to fire at harmless buck," and I believed him. Bivouacked Verdesverdarg.

No. 3210, Private Coles, 15th Hussars, slightly wounded.

No. 3669, Lance-Corporal J. Lusher, died at Bloemfontein of enteric fever.

11TH.—Like many of my comrades, I had foolishly eaten more of my rations the day before than I could afford, and for breakfast had but little left. This morning we crossed the Vaalch River Drift—a very fine one—and were almost immediately sniped at by a few Boers, who took cover among the Kaffir kraals. However, we trotted quietly on to the ridge without casualty, the enemy retiring to a hill some distance away, where they had a gun which shelled us at intervals till nightfall. We did not off-saddle until 8 p.m.

About 9 p.m. we heard several loud explosions in the direction of Kroonstad, and afterwards learned that the railway bridge had been blown up. Bivouacked at Valsch River Drift.

12TH.—Saddled just before dawn and marched some time later. Our advanced squadron came upon a party of about four Burghers bearing a white flag. They were conducted to General French, and our troops occupied the town and camped at Jordon Siding.

In almost every town, small though many of them were, one met English men and women. A Yorkshire lady spoke to me as we passed by to-day and thrust into my hand a loaf of bread in her gratitude at seeing British troops. We had not had any food, I had not, at any rate, since noon the day previous, and that loaf came in very acceptable. To hark back a little, four of us, Regimental-Sergeant-Major Mountford, Farrier-Quartermaster-Sergeant Swarbrick, Trumpeter King, and myself, turned out our pockets and haversacks last night and mustered amongst us two tea tabloids and what would probably be about one and a half biscuits in tiny pieces—a poor tea and supper for four.

13TH.—A rest day much needed by man and horse. Sheep issued for rations. Very little forage for the horses.

14TH.—Orders were received to-day to march at 6 a.m. to-morrow. There were only 93 horses in the regiment fit to travel, viz.:—" A " Squadron, 34 ; " B " Squadron, 34 ; " C " Squadron, 25. A number of men were ordered to " Stand to " ready to return to Bloemfontein for remounts and to take the unfit horses back.

15TH.—Cannot proceed. No forage. Later in the day we were issued with three days' groceries, two days' biscuits, and two days' forage. During these last three days we have had patrols out in a northerly direction, and each time they have been sniped at from the farms dotted here and there about the country. One farm in particular always seemed to be full of Boers. To-day this farm was rushed by a strong patrol of the 14th Hussars, but when taken was found to contain only two men and a large number of women and children. It was well stocked with food and provisions of all kinds. This farm was destroyed and the men brought in to camp. I was sent with an

MAY, 1900.

escort to hand over the prisoners to the authorities at Kroonstad. I mention this because this gave me an opportunity of seeing how Boers behaved when taken prisoners and confined, as these two deserved to be. In the Court House there were a lot of other Boers, who had been equally guilty. Whilst handing the two over I heard more grumbling and complaining than anyone would have thought possible. Their food was not sufficient to satisfy a child's hunger, they were cold (with two blankets each, and a large warm fire), they had only been fighting for their rights, and they added a few choice oaths to emphasise their sorrows.

Extract from "London Gazette":—8th Hussars, Lieutenant P. A. T. Jones to be adjutant, vice Captain C. H. Campbell, who has resigned that appointment.

No. 3967, Private J. Dunn, died at Bloemfontein of cholescystitis.

16TH.—Reveillé 5.30 a.m. Moved camp to-day to 1½ miles nearer to Kroonstad.

17TH AND 18TH.—Remained in the same camp. A number of remounts arrived, under charge of Captain Burns Lindow, and a very scraggy lot they were. After being inspected one-third were declared unfit for duty.

No. 3841, Private J. Brown, died at Bloemfontein of enteric fever.

19TH.—The 14th Hussars were ordered out to destroy several farms close by from which our troops had been fired at yesterday. At 11 p.m. we were issued with two days' rations.

20TH.—Marched at 8 a.m. Our brigade was not as strong as General French would have liked, but it was not to be helped. The remounts, which had been expected to fully horse us, were considered, as mentioned above, unfit to stand the strain of long and tiring marches. The strength of the regiment was 19 officers, 277 men, and 228 horses. To-day we marched about 12 miles and had a good bivouac at night.

MAY, 1900.

21ST.—We heard that Mafeking had been relieved by one of our officers—Colonel B. T. Mahon—in conjunction with Colonel Plumer. Hearty congratulations were heard on all sides for these gallant officers. We halted at night at Welgelegen.

22ND.—The enemy are supposed to be in force on the Rhenoster River and are said to be holding Roodewal Station. After arriving in camp to-day Major Hunter Weston left with an escort furnished by the Scots Greys to endeavour to cut the railway as far north as possible. Conflicting reports were received as to the strength and position of the enemy. Some said that the Boers were exceptionally strong, and held a good position on the Rhenoster, and others that there would be no fighting this side of the Vaal. However, General French, as usual, left nothing to chance, and on the 23rd reveillé was at 1 a.m., and we marched at 2.45 a.m. No smoking or talking was permitted. Half rations of biscuits and tea are all that can be spared now, but fresh meat is to be had in plenty, when there is time on arrival in camp to kill the beasts and cook the beef. The troops, however, do not eat much of this freshly-killed meat, as it is said to assist in bringing on dysentery. It was bitterly cold about this time in the evening after the sun set, until it became strong again the next morning. Nowadays one froze and boiled in turn. Late at night I heard that divisional orders said " The force will cross the Vaal to-morrow." I have since learned that what I heard was not far out, as the wording of the order was:—" General French will cross the Vaal to-morrow." Each evening orders generally ended with " The force will bivouac at ——— to-morrow," and we did. So that for our General to say " We cross the Vaal to-morrow," although looked upon as, lapsing into a slang expression, " a tall order," we fully expected to do so, and we did.

24TH.—Queen's Birthday. A bitterly cold morning. Left camp at daybreak and walked at first to try to get warm. As the sun rose so the weather warmed, and after breaking the ice on a dam to water our horses the whole of the regiment was detailed as an advance guard to proceed to Parys on the Vaal, and after securing the town to cross the river with the least possible delay. The Vaal was very low, and at Parys Drift there were a lot of immense boulders about mid-stream. It was impossible to ride across, and to take wagons or guns across was out of the question. No opposition was met with on entering the town, and the regiment crossed as quickly as possible, and occupied the range of hills overlooking and running parallel to the Vaal some two miles away. Captain Deare and " C " Squadron were the first across about 10.45 a.m. Considering the difficulties which the enemy knew we should have in crossing, the almost sheer bank to be climbed on the opposite side, the long ridge of hills from which guns could have peppered the drift at known distances, it seemed scarcely credible that no opposition was made. Again, on reaching the other side, and whilst trotting up to the ridge, we came across great dongas which would have held thousands of Boers, who could have considerably harassed, and seriously delayed, our crossing. However, nothing occurred, and not a party of Boers was to be seen. During this last hour or two everything seemed to have undergone a great change. From cold and frost to warmth and glorious sunshine, from scarcity of water, and bad at that, to the plenty and beautiful water of the Vaal, and, greatest of all, we had crossed the river and entered the Transvaal on Her Majesty's Birthday—an additional cause for the general rejoicing going on all round. Everyone seemed to have taken a new lease of life. One could not help but notice the look of relief which staff officers and our own officers wore; how the anxious looks of the past few days had disappeared, giving place to looks of quiet and satisfied contentment and determination.

As if to add to the general good humour that prevailed,

MAY, 1900.

the hills for miles around were swept with grass fires, which lit up the country and added their quota by the effective, pretty, and picturesque scene so produced.

25TH.—Reveillé 6 a.m. To-day we did not turn out till 8.50 a.m.—the latest we have turned out as yet. Several shots were fired at us by a few Boers, but no fighting took place, and we halted and camped at Zeekoefontein Spruit, about four miles east of Lindeque, close to the drift.

No. 2742, 15th Hussars, Private A. Seward, attached, died at Bloemfontein of enteric fever.

26TH.—Rose at daybreak, and proceeded to Reitspruit. There was some little fighting on the way, our troops accounting for a Field Cornet killed, among others, besides taking several prisoners. Our casualties to-day were chiefly amongst the Canadians.

27TH.—Reveillé 4 a.m. Moved at daybreak. Enemy were in front, but retired before our advance guard, exchanging a few shots as they did so. Hear to-day that the enemy are retiring on Klip River, where they are said to intend to make a great stand. After going some distance we halted, and General French and his Staff dismounted and apparently took stock of the country before ordering a further advance. Almost as soon as we moved off we were met by a heavy shell and pom-pom fire, the 1st Brigade receiving attention from the enemy first, and afterwards treating us in like manner. The enemy were endeavouring to occupy an angular position, of which on our present line of advance we should have formed the base to complete a triangle. This position blocked our way to the Klipriversberg. The right of this triangle they already held with guns and pom-pom, and were about to occupy the opposite side, but were prevented by the regiment, which galloped up the ridge as far as possible and scrambled up the remainder, just in time to fire a few shots at the enemy, who were too late to seize the ridge.

MAY, 1900.

Early this morning contact squadrons had been sent out, " B " Squadron proceeding to Hout Kop and " A " Squadron to Meyerton Station. General French highly complimented the squadrons on their day's work. To-day had been a long and tiring one.

28TH.—We had not proceeded far when we heard from the enemy on the Klipriversberg. We halted at a farm, from which we looted a large quantity of good forage. A big gun on the Berg tried to reach us, but the shells fell about 200 yards short.

Advancing later we moved in a northerly direction parallel to the Boer position, and after proceeding, I should think, about four miles, bringing us towards his right flank, we wheeled to our right in an endeavour, I believe, to find if we had reached his flank or else to make a demonstration to make our foe show his hand. We certainly did not strike the flank, but we did strike the hottest fire we had been under so far. " O " Battery came into action, but it was of no avail, and they were ordered to limber up. The brigade wheeled to its right and trotted along the front of the Boer position by regiments in line of squadron column. Big gun and pom-pom fire was launched at us, and shells fell thickly among the troops. The pom-poms were unable to quite reach us, their shells falling about 200 yards short of the left flank.

When we were nearing the end of our ride we encountered a heavy rifle and pom-pom fire. Finally we wheeled to our right and halted out of range. Colonel Clowes ordered the non-commissioned officers of troops to call their rolls to find the total losses in the regiment. It seemed incredible to hear that none were missing, and that only one had been wounded. " B " Squadron, with " O " Battery, came in for a worse time, I think, than we had done, but, as wonderful to relate, without any casualties. The pace at which we moved was that of a steady trot. There was no crowding in the ranks, the men kept well opened out, and there was no confusion. This ride

MAY, 1900.

was witnessed by the Johannesburg people from the Boer position on the Rand near the mines. "The Standard and Diggers' News," of which I afterwards obtained a copy, had for the head-lines describing this:—" French's Cavalry Routed," "The Field Strewed with Dead and Dying," " Boer Ambulances at Work." No doubt from what he saw at a distance, the correspondent responsible for these sensational head-lines felt himself quite justified in presuming that such must be the inevitable result of these last operations. Happily, he was very far from the truth. General sympathy was felt throughout the brigade for Major Mackeson, who rode with General Dickson at the head of the column, and who was severely wounded in the face, and for Sergeant McGavish, of " O " Battery, who was struck in the body by a shell, and, of course, instantly killed. One of their big guns had been paying attention to our convoy, but only one shell had any effect, and that only took the side out of an ammunition wagon. We retired for the night to our last night's bivouac—our first retirement.

3540 Private Routledge, wounded.

29TH.—Enemy still occupy the same position as yesterday. I should estimate their line of front at from seven miles. To-day we were reinforced by General Ian Hamilton's Brigade, C.I.V., Gordons, and Mounted Infantry. " O " Battery were successful in causing the enemy to retire from a small kopje about the centre of their position, and which we at once occupied.

30TH.—Reveillé 4.45 a.m. An artillery duel commenced almost with the break of day and lasted hours. During the day the Gordons charged the kopje on which the enemy had a big gun, and were repulsed on two occasions with heavy losses, but succeeded at the third attempt, losing their gallant colonel, and having a very heavy casualty list. Our brigade now moved further north, and when nearing Dorn Kop, celebrated in the Jameson Raid, the Boers were observed to be moving in

MAY, 1900.

that direction also, and with either a gun or a pompom. In the race for this kopje the 1st and 4th Cavalry Brigades managed to reach it just in time to prevent the Boers unlimbering, and our pom-pom coming rapidly into action, and making excellent practice, proceeded to pour such a heavy fire into them that they retired. It was now dusk, and we camped on the ground we had won, or, to be more accurate, we camped at the foot of it, our outposts occupying the kop itself.

31ST.—Reveillé 4.45 a.m. Marched at daybreak from the foot of Dorn Kop and on to the Rand—a broad, level plain across which the enemy had retired during the evening and night of yesterday. As we crossed the plain we came across the tracks made by the enemy in his retirement. We found one dead Boer and one wounded on the route taken by our brigade. The first mentioned had been shot by a bullet which had passed through the brass case of one of the bullets in his bandolier, and which had afterwards entered the body—in all probability the shot from the effects of which he had eventually succumbed whilst riding away. We reached the Rand Mines and halted for a time. The railway runs past these direct to Johannesburg, which is ten miles away. After a short halt we moved in the direction of Driefontein, where a portion of the enemy's convoy had halted. Our troops captured a Creusot gun, seven wagons, and several prisoners. I saw a large Boer spent shell strike a man of the artillery on the arm as it fell, but, beyond causing a large and painful bruise, it did no further damage to him. Major Wood shortly afterwards had a narrow escape from a serious accident, his horse dragging him some distance along the ground by the stirrup until his foot became disengaged.

1ST JUNE.—Reveillé 6 a.m. Klipfontein. To-day was a rest day. The Union Jack was hoisted in Johannesburg at 10.30 this morning. In camp the troops indulged

JUNE, 1900.

in a wash, shave, and a clean change—three luxuries which were heartily enjoyed.

2ND.—To-day's was a short march. On reaching camp we drew two days' rations and supplies, seven biscuits per man for two days, and horses 5lbs. of corn per day. From this camp—Waterval—Major Wood was admitted to hospital at Johannesburg with a damaged ankle, the result of the accident referred to on the 1st inst.

3RD.—To-day we marched to the junction of the Crocodile and Hartebeesthoek Rivers. The regiment crossed without opposition. Many of the troops helped themselves to bundles of forage from a farm building soon after crossing. About noon our advance guard saw, only about three miles away, a large Boer convoy passing from west to east, right across our front. We were nothing like strong enough to even drive in its escort, which held a strong position on a rocky ridge. It was most exasperating to see the wagons moving slowly along, to see the Kaffirs urging on the cattle, and our chances of a bag gradually fading away as time passed on, and no assistance came. In two hours' time, when it did arrive, we were too late. Evening began to set in, but, pressing on, we came to a narrow pass, through which the 1st Brigade, who were leading, essayed to enter. The leading section reached the jaw of the pass, when they were saluted with a sudden and heavy rifle fire, and all were unhorsed. Then commenced a fusilade which lasted until late at night. Back from the pass lay a long ridge, which was strongly held by Boer riflemen. General French was almost on top of the advance guard, and certainly but very few yards behind the section which was shot down—the section had closed in as it was impossible for them to advance without so doing. We had not expected opposition here. The troops were all sixes and sevens, troops, convoy, and artillery were all mixed up when the first salute was received from the enemy. In almost less than the time it takes to write this our General must have taken in the situation. The guns were ordered up together with the pom-poms.

The gallant gunners give marvellous displays of their rapidity in coming into action at exhibitions at home. I never timed such, but if they can get into action quicker than they did at Dorn Kop and again to-day, I should like to be present to see it. But this is a digression.

Everyone seemed to keep his head. Everything seemed to be taken as a matter of course. There was no confusion. The dispositions were quickly made, officers and men seemed to anticipate their orders, and soon we were more than holding our own. The noise was deafening, guns, pom-poms, Mauser, and our own fire—one continuous roar—roars which were echoed and re-echoed amongst the hills.

Our General determined to assault the ridge, and a Colonial Corps—the Canadians—and the Carabiniers from the 1st Brigade, dismounted, and for once cavalry took the place of our infantry comrades, and right well they did it, too. It was almost too dark to see them climbing the ridge, which was black in itself, but before it was quite dark we held the ridge in front of us on each side of the pass. Boer losses, 20 killed; ours, 8 killed. It was a lucky thing for "A" Squadron that day, I believe, that for a short time during the afternoon they had wandered a little too far east, otherwise they would have met the enemy without any support at hand, and I should have had a different chronicle to write of to-day's events. The squadron, however, captured several prisoners, and re-joined the brigade very late at night. This camp was called Kalkheuvel. Our bivouac to-night was in a farm yard. There was no regular system of bivouacking, as on other nights, everyone dumping down anywhere and making the best of what we had. My experience to-night was anything but pleasant. We had been served out with an issue of flour on the previous day, and to-night, as soon as we had settled down a little, I lit a fire and made my

JUNE, 1900

flour ration into small chupatties; that is I made little cakes of flour and water mixed and fried in fat. I ate a couple, and placed the remainder in my haversack, and went to get a drink of water from a small spruit close by. On returning I found my horse just finishing the last chupattie, and, of course, with it all my food for the next day.

4TH.—First thing this morning our troops buried a number of the Boers found on the ridges, at the foot of which, on the opposite side, and on the road, we found two Boer ambulances and several wounded men with a Boer doctor. After proceeding some distance we came across a farm, in the grounds of which was a very long table, on which had been laid a repast for our retreating enemy. Opposite to this farm was an orange grove full of ripe oranges. What a feed we had. I felt able to forgive my horse for his theft of the previous night. The tangerines were specially sweet and plentiful. We carried away as many as we could, stowing them away in every available space on our person or accoutrements. We had splendid bivouac at night near the bridge over the Crocodile River, near General Schuman's Farm.

5TH.—We rose early, and marching in a N.E. direction, entered Ziligats Nek on the Magalisberg, through which range of hills we passed without opposition, having another good feed of oranges from the groves on the line of march.

6TH.—A most eventful day. We moved eastwards towards a commanding fort on the Magaliesberg-Wonderboom Fort. "C" Squadron, under Captain Deare, was sent to reconnoitre the pass at the foot of the fort. They found pass and fort occupied by the Norfolk Regiment, and the guns removed, and were the first to obtain a view of Pretoria, which could be plainly seen but a short distance away. The 4th Cavalry Brigade came to within half a mile wide of the pass and halted, whilst the

JUNE, 1900.

1st Brigade proceeded in the direction of Waterval, where the Boers had their prisoners. These were guarded by only a small escort, which was soon overcome, and retired. After retiring to a commando which was on a ridge some distance away these "poor, peaceful, and harmless farmers" commenced to blaze away with four guns at the defenceless prisoners, and several were severely wounded, one or two fatally—a sad fate at the moment of release after probably months of captivity, and after suffering such privations as fall to the lot of those so unfortunate to be taken by such an enemy.

A message from Colonel Porter, just received, says that 36 or 16 officers (my entry is now not quite plain), and 3,500 men had been released, and asked for trains to take them into Pretoria. We remained halted at this spot, which was close to the line, long enough to see the first train load, in open trucks, come through. It is unnecessary to say how pleased the men were to see us, or we to see them. About noon we prepared to enter Pretoria. We marched through Wonderboom Fort, and in a short time we entered the town. On the way several Burghers stopped Colonel Clowes, who was leading the regiment, and requested him to cause them to be supplied with the copy of a Proclamation, which they said they had heard had been published re terms to Burghers who were willing to surrender.

7TH.—Next morning was quiet. One did not feel that there was any war knocking about. It seemed rather that one might conclude that now Pretoria was occupied the war was over. At noon, however, we were suddenly ordered out to proceed to a range of hills close by, as what was supposed to be a Boer commando was reported approaching. "B" Squadron proceeded mounted, the remainder dismounted. We remained there until late in the afternoon, when we were relieved without having seen any sign of Boers. Staff-Sergeant-Farrier Asher re-joined to-day. He had been out in South Africa since

15th September, 1899. A number of Burghers came in under a white flag to-day and surrendered.
No. 4046, Lance-Corporal G. Hunter, died at Bloemfontein of enteric fever.

8TH.—Marched at 10 a.m. through Derdeport and Kameeldrift, and bivouacked at Zeekoegat. On our way there we saw the enemy shelling our last night's camping ground. Our artillery replied, and they soon ceased.

9TH.—Reveillé 5 a.m. We were first ordered to move at 6 a.m. back to our last camp. After saddling and standing to for a time we off-saddled and "stood to." To-day was beautifully fine after the severe thunderstorm which we experienced last night. A small issue was made to-day of sugar, coffee, baking powder, rice, and bread.

10TH.—A number of sick horses left for Silverton.

11TH.—Marched at daybreak towards Kameelfontein. I can safely assert, I think, that when we left camp that morning few of us had any idea that such a large Boer force was close at hand as we afterwards encountered. The 1st and 4th Cavalry Brigades marched in the same direction, 4th Cavalry Brigade leading. Soon after crossing a drift we heard from our enemy. The regiment was ordered to wheel to the right and occupy a ridge. We did so. The led horses were being removed to a place of shelter, but the leading file took the wrong direction, and offered a fine target to the enemy, who immediately opened fire with a pom-pom, and had it not been for Squadron-Sergeant-Major Stretch perceiving the mistake many casualties must have occurred. As it was, the direction was immediately altered, and we got into comparative safety with the loss of Private Nelson, of French's Scouts, attached to the regiment, wounded by a pom-pom shell, which burst just behind him, many pieces of which entered his back; the pieces from this shell also severely wounded Lieutenant P. A. T. Jones's horse. The regiment held this ridge from about 8 a.m. to-day, the 11th inst., until about the same hour on the 13th, without

SOUTH AFRICAN WAR

JUNE, 1900.

being relieved. It was then found that the enemy had retired during the night of the 12th. During these 48 hours the men were very short of food and water. The good cover afforded by the rocks and large boulders assisted in preventing a large casualty list, only Captain O'Brien being severely wounded and Sergeant Appleton slightly so. During these two days water was carried up to the troops in water bottles, and the horses watered at night at a spruit about a mile and a half away. This spruit and the road leading to it was periodically shelled by the Boers.

Lieutenant O'Brien severely wounded shoulder.

Private Nelson, French's Scouts, severely wounded thigh.

No. 3297, Sergeant C. Appleton, slightly wounded left fore-arm.

13TH.—On the morning of the 13th it was surmised that the Boers had abandoned the positions they had been holding, and Lieutenant Jones and Squadron-Sergeant-Major Burns reconnoitred these positions on foot, and found them clear of the enemy. We then proceeded to our convoy, which was some three miles to our rear, and after obtaining supplies we bivouacked late at night on a camping ground which must have been quite recently occupied by the enemy, as several of the fires were still burning slightly.

14TH.—We marched to-day to Kameel-Drift, about nine miles north of Pretoria.

15TH.—The brigade received a visit from General French, who complimented it on the excellent work it had done since leaving Bloemfontein.

Captain H. N. Thoyts and Lieutenant Jennings admitted to hospital at Pretoria.

17TH.—Lieutenant and Quartermaster Page invalided from Bloemfontein and embarked at Capetown for England.

We were encamped on fairly good ground, but the wind

JUNE, 1900.

blew plenty of sand about, and oftentimes made things very uncomfortable. Tents were not available, and we made blanket shelters, and were fairly comfortable in that respect. Sometimes we suffered from heavy rains and sometimes from sand-storms. Everyone now utilised his spare time in washing and repairing his clothing and in writing letters home. The horses were out grazing daily.

No. 2736, Private J. Stevens, 15th Hussars, attached, died at Bloemfontein of enteric fever.

20TH.—Horse parade. An outbreak of glanders was discovered in "O" Battery, in consequence of which on the 21st we moved our camp across the drift and about a mile away from the battery. Before we could get settled down a heavy fall of rain commenced, and continued the whole night. Happily this was not accompanied by high winds, or our temporarily erected shelters would have been blown away. As it was, we had to walk about during the greater part of the night. One squadron ("A") was out on outpost duty.

22ND.—Fine but cold. I rigged up a fine bivouac to-day, which lasted until we moved out of this camp on the 9th of July.

24TH.—Mails arrived.

25TH.—One squadron on outpost duty.

26TH.—Many non-commissioned officers and men proceeded to Pretoria chiefly to view the museum.

No. 3210, Private J. Coles, 15th Hussars, attached, died at Bloemfontein of enteric fever.

No. 4553, Private W. Brown, died at Bloemfontein of enteric fever.

27TH.—It was published officially in orders that De Wet had destroyed about three weeks' mails which all had been anxiously awaiting.

28TH.—Ordered to saddle up in marching order at 6 a.m. Various reports of Boer activity. We did not, however, leave camp.

29TH.—Exercise. During the day Lieutenant G. M.

SOUTH AFRICAN WAR

JUNE, 1900.

Mort and Lieutenant C. C. Wilson, Westmoreland and Cumberland Yeomanry, re-joined from hospital and Cavalry Depôt, Bloemfontein, respectively. Second-Lieutenant Lord Hindlip joined the regiment with the following draft of 30 3rd Hussars Reservists:—

Thirty Reservists, 3rd Hussars, posted to regiment:—

2951	Lce.-Cpl. Beale.	3072	Pte. Kennedy.
2826	Pte. Deadman.	3106	Pte. Kelly.
2758	Pte. Langston.	3939	Pte. Moody.
2833	Pte. Hulme.	2829	Pte. Platt.
2585	Pte. Bittlestone.	2733	Pte. Thorogood.
2641	Pte. Taylor.	2677	Pte. Bolding.
2862	Pte. Black.	2694	Pte. Dafter.
3027	Pte. Crow.	2923	Pte. Holt.
2950	Pte. Gardner.	3243	Pte. Lewes.
3197	Pte. Cornwall.	2817	Pte. Pugh.
3143	Pte. Armstrong.	2842	Pte. Ballard.
3251	Lce.-Cpl. Cross.	2727	Pte. Hileds.
2551	Pte. Bawcutt.	2865	Pte. Kitchener.
2739	Pte. Bennett.	2814	Pte. Knowles.
2919	Pte. Bowling.	2718	Pte. Matthews.

30TH.—Another alarm parade which came to nothing.

2ND JULY.—Saddled at 6 a.m., but did not leave camp. We received orders, however, to be ready to move at any time and at very short notice. Lieutenant Hon. M. F. Howard, Second-Lieutenant E. G. Woods, Second-Lieutenant L. G. Scott, and Second-Lieutenant Sir R. W. Levinge joined with the following draft:—

Draft, under Second-Lieutenant Woods, arrived from England. Disembarked at Capetown, ex s.s. "Cavour," 13th June, 1900, and composed of:—

2739	15th Hussars, Lce.-Sgt. Cunningham.	2622	15th Hussars, Pte. Gilbert.
3081	Cpl. Horne.	4213	Pte. Brady.
2997	15th Hussars, Cpl. Forsdike.	3361	Pte. Brown.
		4585	Pte. Burns.
3107	15th Hussars, Cpl. Morse.	4209	Pte. Dawson.
4180	Pte. Dignan.	4467	Pte. Dunn.
4421	Pte. Doyle.	4268	Pte. Edwards.
2621	15th Hussars, Pte. Gilbert.	4411	Pte. Ewan.
		4564	Pte. Farmer.

JULY, 1900.

4306	Pte.	Fawcett.	4431	Pte.	Walsh.
4456	Pte.	Gibbons.	4368	Pte.	Wilson.
4438	Pte.	Greely.	2946	15th Hussars, Pte.	**Scrogie**
4272	Pte.	Harper.	3741	Pte.	Parris.
4224	Pte.	Holland.	3739	Pte.	Scott.
4326	Pte.	Brunton.	3310	**Pte.**	**Davey.**
4486	Pte.	Merrigan.	4450	Pte.	Farrell.
3923	Pte.	Gill.	4413	Pte.	Chubb.
4333	Pte.	Holian.	3053	15th Hussars, Pte.	Hillier.
4405	Pte.	Horton.	2870	15th Hussars, Pte.	Parks.
4302	Pte.	Jurdison.	2578	15th Hussars, Pte.	Cole.
4159	Pte.	Kennedy.	2905	**15th Hussars, Pte.**	**Prest.**
4188	Pte.	Keogh.	2543	**15th Hussars, Pte.**	**Priest.**
4354	Pte.	Lee.	2660	15th Hussars, Pte.	Wells.
4273	Pte.	Laird.	3655	Pte.	Keating.
4620	Pte.	Lyons.	4248	Pte.	Lockwell.
4305	Pte.	McKay.	3434	Pte.	Kidney.
4344	Pte.	Moulds	4354	Pte. Keating joined from England with Sec.-Lieut. Hindlip.	
4244	Pte.	Payne.			
4332	Pte.	Roache.			

To-day all foreigners who had not taken the oath of allegiance were sent out of Pretoria to East London. The townspeople of Pretoria are now settling down to the ordinary routine of life, shops are being opened again, and food stuffs are obtainable at prices something like the following:—Per pound: Rice 6d., sugar 6d., bread 6d., jam 1s. 3d. a small tin. Butter was not obtainable at any price.

We have now about 80 horses per squadron.

4TH.—A number of remounts arrived yesterday and to-day, and a parade in drill order was ordered to accustom them to leaving the ranks.

5TH.—Parade in drill order. The average squadron strength to-day is 127 non-commissioned officers and men and 106 horses. A quantity of stores and clothing arrived and was issued. To-night was very cold.

6TH.—General French visited the camp and inspected the horses. He inquired carefully into the quantity and quality of the forage issued for each horse.

7TH.—One squadron turned out at 3.30 p.m. to make a

JULY, 1900.

reconnaissance. Heavy gun fire heard from an easterly direction during the afternoon.

8TH.—The squadron out yesterday returned at 9.30 a.m. to-day. To vary the monotony we played the 14th Hussars a cricket match this afternoon, using pick handles for bats. Scores: 14th, 45; 8th, 59.

9TH.—Further stores were to be drawn to-day, but a sudden order was received about 8.30 to parade at 10 a.m. We marched, as ordered, towards Reitfontein, south-east of Pretoria, reaching camp—Reitvlei—about 8 p.m. It was dark long before this hour, and many lost their way, and did not join us till quite late.

10TH.—Continued the march and reached General Hutton's camp at Reitfontein, close to which he had been constantly engaged during the last four days. Soon after arriving in camp the officers of the Royal Fusiliers and the officers of the Connaught Rangers, whose regiments formed a portion of the forces engaged, helioed in to our regiment congratulating us on our march up country, and saying that it gave all ranks great pleasure to have the 8th Hussars fighting by their side. At night a big veldt fire nearly overcame our efforts to put it out, causing much concern in camp.

11TH.—Under the command of Colonel Porter, the 1st Cavalry Brigade, of which we formed part, moved early this morning towards the enemy's left flank, and soon came across their outpost line, which, at the point we engaged them, was on a long flat ridge—Leukop—which was capable of being ridden up. Opening out, "B" Squadron, led by Captain Mussenden, occupied this by proceeding at a steady trot, with the loss of one—Scout Shepherd—killed. We remained on this ridge all day, being ineffectively shelled by two long range guns, one in front of us and one on our right. A large proportion of the regiment occupied an extended outpost line to-night, the remainder and the convoy camped at Olifantsfontein.

12TH.—The convoy remained in camp, and the whole

JULY, 1900.

regiment proceeded to strengthen the line of outposts. There was but little firing to-day, but the enemy were known to be occupying the same positions as yesterday.

13TH.—Same dispositions as yesterday. I had an opportunity of visiting the farm to-day, in the grounds of which, near the house, were scattered ghastly evidences of the destructive power of the shells of our artillery. Some days previously our gunners had directed their fire in this direction, where a number of Boers—possibly a picquet—were located. A large shell had passed through the trunk of this tree and had burst with terrific force on emerging, blowing men and horses into fragments. Pieces of men, clothing, and horses were scattered about in all directions. I afterwards saw a very good and true picture of this tree in the London "Daily Graphic." So possibly many of my readers also saw the tree, which was of considerable width round the trunk.

14TH AND 15TH.—Same camp and routine. On the 15th a 4.7 gun was sent to Leukop to strengthen the position.

16TH.—Early this morning the enemy drove in our cossack posts, and the whole brigade left camp, and a general engagement commenced all along the line of the brigades engaged—a line about 15 miles long. Colonel Clowes, with the 8th Hussars, held the right of the line. On and beyond the right of the line the country became flat, and a party of the enemy endeavoured to occupy a small kopje which would command the flank. This was prevented by "B" Squadron, who galloped and reached it just in time. This kopje was out of rifle range from the enemy's position, but they used gun and pom-pom fire in an effort to dislodge the squadron, without effect. The shrapnel used burst too high to do any damage. Had they been able to burst their shells the position would not have been tenable. As it was, however, their attempt to flank the right was a failure.

SOUTH AFRICAN WAR

JULY, 1900.

General Hutton gave Colonel Clowes full power, a helio message saying that the flank must be held at all costs.

No. 3079, Private H. Wale, injured at Reitvlei by fall from a horse.

17TH.—Occupied the same positions as yesterday, but, although Boers could be seen moving along their positions, they did not open fire. We learned that yesterday's attack was intended to act simultaneously with a rising that was to take place at the same time in Johannesburg, which, however, fell through. This was about the first time in our experience that the enemy had opened such a determined attack. A flag of truce came in to us offering safe escort to a party to go to bury our dead. The regiment returned to camp later in the day, and was immediately ordered to proceed, under command of Major Duff, as escort to a convoy proceeding to Springs for rations and stores. The convoy consisted of 90 bullock wagons, and a miserable ride through the night it was conducting them.

No. 2916, Private R. Tudguy, 15th Hussars, attached, died at Johannesberg of enteric fever.

18TH.—Stores were drawn and loaded. The warm British coats were issued to the regiment during the loading of the convoy. We commenced our return journey at 4 p.m., and travelled through the night again. It was freezing keenly, but the veldt fires which were burning in all directions tempered the severity somewhat. Arrived in camp at Olifantsfontein about 6.30 a.m.

19TH.—The regiment drew stores, etc., and received the presents of tobacco and socks sent out to us from the depôt at home. The 4th Cavalry Brigade arrived at Olifantsfontein to-day. We are to rejoin them when we march from this camp. Since the regiment left them at Kameel Drift " O " Battery and the 7th Dragoon Guards had sustained severe losses.

20TH AND 22ND.—Remained in camp. I may here remark it was about as miserable a camp as one could find. There was no grass on the ground, and high winds prevailed, dust storms being a source of great discomfort.

23RD.—Marched at daybreak, carrying as little as possible on the saddles. Warm British coats left behind. Three days' rations carried on the man and two on the horse. "A" Squadron, in a thick fog, reconnoitred position recently held by Boers, and found it vacated. After proceeding about four miles we came across the enemy, and an artillery duel commenced and lasted some time. The regiment was detached from the brigade, and acted under the immediate orders of General French; squadrons and troops being despatched at various times on reconnoitring duties. The artillery fire lasted until nightfall, but we maintained a steady advance, and when hostilities for the day ceased we joined the 4th Cavalry Brigade at Deeplaagte in a miserable bivouac where neither wood nor water could be found.

24TH.—Saddled at daybreak. The regiment was again under the immediate orders of General French, who instructed Colonel Clowes to cause it to form line with the men riding at intervals of about 50 yards, and in this manner keep touch with General Hutton's Brigade on the left of the cavalry brigades who were in force on the right of an extended line. The enemy were thus gradually driven back, and General Hutton gradually closed on the cavalry brigades. Thus relieved, the regiment concentrated, and was again used for special patrolling, etc. The Boers made a protracted stand on a long ridge. Colonel Alderson, with his mounted infantry, was now on our left. About 4 p.m. Lieutenant C. C. Wilson, Westmoreland and Cumberland Yeomanry, attached, who was out with a patrol, under Captain Deare, "C" Squadron, at a farm house close to the Boer position, was severely wounded in thigh and stomach, but was well treated by the Boer farmers, and a small patrol of the enemy who came down from the ridge. Camped at Waterpan.

25TH.—Marched at daybreak with the 1st Brigade. It

JULY, 1900.

is evident that the main body of the enemy are in retreat, and that they have left a rear guard with a long Tom to cover them. This gun fired incessantly, but did no damage. Towards evening we crossed the river at Naauwport Drift and bivouacked. Before the regiment could get picketed down heavy rains came on, and men and horses were soaked. It was a bitter cold night, and lying out in the open on a wet ground and in wet blankets was not conducive to one's health. I am sorry to record that to-night an officer and three men of the Argyll and Sutherland Highlanders, died from exposure—a sad death.

No. 2552, Private, J. Regan, missing; subsequently rejoined.

26TH.—A day's work similar to that of yesterday. The rear guard was more determined to-day, a dismounted party endeavouring to prevent the advance of our troops up a long gradual slope which led to the crest of a ridge.

A bog lay at the foot, and they doubtless hoped for some profitable sniping should any of the troops become stuck. The presence of the bog was discovered in plenty of time to prevent this, and Johnny Boer retired under cover of his Long Tom. Bivouacked at Sterkwater.

27TH.—Reveillé 6 a.m. Again the Boers retired in front of us towards the railway. We met with but little opposition until close to Pan Station. From the far side of the ridge of a large "pan" we could see the enemy retiring on the line and firing the gun to prevent our advance, assisted by a skirmishing line.

"C" Squadron advanced at a trot, and caused their hasty departure by rail, with the loss of No. 4337, Private Wade, 16th Lancers, attached, wounded when quite close to the station. I found to-day how easy it is to lose one's way. Just prior to the squadron advancing I had been taking a message for the General from the 14th Hussars, who were some miles to our right rear, and Colonel Clowes had, as I thought, gone after the squadron.

JULY, 1900.

After packing up I trotted after him, but on passing Sergeant Joice with the machine gun section I was told that the colonel had not accompanied the squadron, so I started back again. Before going far I met with clouds of smoke from a veldt fire, and soon I was uncertain which way to proceed. However, I picked a part where the smoke was thinnest, rode through it, and found the regiment, after half an hour, being close on the advance guard of " A " Squadron, concealed amongst some rocks, almost before I saw them.

Very few of the regiment reached the camp at Erfdeil that night.

Lieutenant Lambert and Sergeant Joice went out to-night to destroy a portion of the railway east of Pan Station to prevent the return of the enemy by rail. They were successful, and returned to camp next morning.

28TH.—Remained in camp.

29TH.—Moved camp about two or three miles to Lemoenfontein nearer to the railway. General Hutton is again on our left. A helio message informed us that Middleburg was occupied on 26th inst.

30TH.—Information circulated that General Prinsloo and a large number of Boers had been captured or surrendered down country. Lieutenant Van der Byl, " C " Squadron, out with a patrol, encountered a small body of the enemy. The patrol was compelled to split up, and returned to camp minus three men, and two horses which had been shot.

No. 4293, Lance-Corporal Perugia, 16th Lancers, attached, killed in action whilst on patrol duty near Wonderfontein Station.

31ST.—Missing men re-joined, having luckily avoided being taken by enemy.

1ST AUGUST.—A party of about only 40 Boers opposed our march to-day, our objective being Wonderfontein Station. When close to the line a timely dash of a patrol of " C " Squadron, under Sergeant Parry, seized the

AUGUST, 1900.

station before the small Boer opposition could reach a cutting close by and prevent them.

Regiment bivouacked about 1½ miles south of line.

"C" Squadron was detached from regiment, and camped at Leeuwfontein, about five miles away, near the line towards Middleburg.

3RD.—Our troops occupy the railway cutting north-east of the station during the day, and the Boers regularly do the same at night after our picquet retires. Their patrols are to be seen moving about daily, several slight skirmishes taking place yesterday and to-day, when Private Ayres was wounded in foot and taken prisoner.

4TH.—To-day one of our patrols was almost captured, having Private Jones, 16th Lancers, attached, wounded.

The Boer patrol is commanded by a Field Cornet, who rides a grey pony. My diary states that this patrol has been left behind to give General Botha full particulars of all the movements of General French's Cavalry Brigade, the whole of which is camped about this part. I believe that this was told to me by the stationmaster at Wonder-fontein, and from the activity of this Field Cornet and his patrol I should say that he misses few of the movements of the troops he has been detailed to watch.

5TH.—To-day our observation post at the cutting was driven in, and No. 4072, Private J. McCormack, 8th Hussars, dangerously wounded.

6TH.—Captain O'Brien was invalided home to-day from Pretoria, the result of the wounds received at Diamond Hill. A portion of General Hutton's Brigade took over the station.

No. 3823, Corporal Hodgetts, embarked at Capetown on s.s. "Ranee" as escort to Boer prisoners, en route to Ceylon.

8TH.—Another skirmish near the station, during which No. 2641, Private G. Taylor, 3rd Hussars, attached, was killed.

E

AUGUST, 1900.

No. 3705, Private G. Abear, died at Germiston, accidentally shot.

9TH.—No. 4072, Private J. McCormack, died from the wounds received on the 5th inst.

12TH.—It is rumoured that a strong Boer force had been despatched to endeavour to re-take Wonderfontein Station. The regiment stood to arms all night. Nothing happened.

13TH.—Lieutenant Jennings embarked at Capetown for Ceylon with Boer prisoners. This officer was detailed for this duty in the hope that during the voyage he would recuperate his health, which had quite broken down during the strain of constant work since 2nd October, 1899.

During our stay in this camp our signallers were worked day and night.

We received and transmitted more messages than we had done during the whole of our journey from Bloemfontein.

15TH.—About 10 o'clock last night I received a message to the effect that we were to move at 10 a.m. to-morrow. It was, however, 3 p.m. before we moved in a south-east direction, and encamped at Strathrae, where we lay between the 14th Hussars and 6th Inniskillings—both good old comrades.

16TH.—General Buller's troops close to us. Their convoy crossed our front to-day en route to Wonderfontein for supplies. We all remarked what splendid condition his horses and cattle were in.

17TH.—Moved to Klippan, close by, recently occupied by General Gordon's 1st Cavalry Brigade.

20TH.—No. 4798, Private Goldsmith, accidentally shot himself to-day—wound not serious.

21ST.—Marched to Blesbock Spruit, where we camped. Fires strewn about show that the enemy have but recently retired.

23RD.—Marched to and bivouacked at Geluk, near to

AUGUST, 1900.

Belfast, about five miles from the railway station. The forces under the direct command of Lord Roberts, of which, of course, we were part, came in touch to-day with the forces under General Buller for the first time. General Buller was about two miles to our right, and General Pole Carew's force on our left at, and about, Belfast Station. We were being very well rationed about this time; better than at any time since we left Bloemfontein, except during our stay at Kameeldrift. De Wet and Steyn are reported to have gone to Machadodorp. I do not know if the presence of such a large body of our troops being about us, or what it was that influenced our opinions, but, with few exceptions, all seemed confident that the war would be over before many more weeks had run out. How wrong we were!

24TH.—Heavy firing to-day on both flanks. The Boers and British forces are about five miles apart. Boer patrols were moving about towards the centre of our position, but they soon retired. Moved our camp two miles nearer to Belfast.

25TH.—I was sent out to-day with a troop as escort to put General Pole Carew's and General Buller's forces in communication with each other by helio. Succeeded.

During the afternoon a large number of wounded and sick from General Buller's force passed by our camp on their way to the station at Belfast to be conveyed to hospital.

26TH.—Moved with the 4th Cavalry Brigade to Belfast and halted for a time on a grassy patch of ground close to the station. It was early morning, and the grass was quite damp. Our regiment had orders not to permit the horses to nibble the grass. Why, was soon discovered. Several horses of the 7th Dragoon Guards were permitted to graze, and almost immediately developed symptoms of poisoning, and died.

The brigade moved later, north of the station, and, after crossing several drifts and bad patches of ground covered

E 2

AUGUST, 1900.

with stones and boulders, we were ordered to occupy a long kopje. We rode in column parallel with the kopje for a time, and on wheeling to our left, found the ground close to the kopje to be bog. Boer snipers in plenty occupied the ridge, but they were too impatient to give us time to get close up, and commenced potting away, consequently we were lucky to get out of range with only one casualty, No. 3719, Saddler J. Louis, severely wounded. This is the second time he has been so unlucky. To assist our retirement, " O " Battery came into action at 1,000 yards, and, as usual, fired with splendid precision. Halting out of rifle range, the battery and our Maxim were both very effective, and we camped there on the worst bit of ground we had struck for a camp so far—without wood and without water.

27TH.—Saddled at daybreak. Firing commenced almost immediately. The enemy gradually retired, and we bivouacked near Lakensvlei Farm, on the left of the general advance on Dalmanutha.

28TH.—Marched at 8 a.m. Travelled first north, then east, then south-east. Small parties of Boers on the kopjes. To-day's march was through a difficult bit of country. After bivouacking the Boers sniped the camp, but were soon silenced by our strong outpost line. Machadodorp and Dalmanutha were occupied to-day by General Buller's forces.

29TH.—We marched at daybreak in a thick fog through an increasingly mountainous country. We led our horses to-day more miles than we rode them. The first height was so difficult that only a section abreast could ascend the mountain pass. It was bitterly cold, but we were warm enough. I am not sure, but I suppose it must have been through the exertion, that caused a trooper of the 17th Lancers to drop, and he was found to be dead when picked up. Later in the day we came to the level ground near to Helvetia, where we again met General Buller's forces. The cavalry brigades watered by

AUGUST, 1900.

regiments at a large dam, and formed up in the open. The enemy had a pom-pom and a small force on a ridge on our left, and by way of diversion they let go with a full belt (25) of pom-pom shells at the 1st Cavalry Brigade. They had no time for more, as, quickly mounting, one regiment was after them, but they just managed to elude capture. Camped at Helvetia, sniping lasting until it was quite dark.

30TH.—We only went a short distance before we found the same snipers, who, however, did no damage. After proceeding to the edge of the plateau which overlooked Watervalonder we halted, and the regiment was detailed to hold this and two conical shaped kopjes on the left. Later, Captain Greathed, from one of the kopjes, sent down a message to the effect that a large number of men were approaching Watervalonder under a white flag. These turned out to be the poor unfortunate British troops who had been in captivity at Nooitgedacht.

I use the word captivity advisedly, because from the weak and emaciated condition of the officers, non-commissioned officers, and men, they had certainly not been properly treated as prisoners of war, but more like captives were treated in the olden days. The excuse that they could not have been better fed, etc., hardly holds water, because months after the idea was quite exploded that the Boers had ever been short of either food or clothing. Altogether about 1,800 were released. As the men passed us on the way to our brigade convoy for food, I had a chance of seeing and conversing with several. They stated how they had been treated and fed, and that General Botha had addressed them before release, saying that he hoped the war would soon be over, etc. The whole of the prisoners were not released; a number, chiefly yeomanry, being taken with the retreating commando.

Horses were placed on half rations to-day. We returned to last night's camping ground.

AUGUST, 1900.

31ST.—Started at 9 a.m. for Machadodorp. A short day's march. Bivouacked in a very dirty camp which had recently been a Boer encampment. I cannot say where the idea came from, but one and all were under the impression that we were now to proceed to Pretoria, and from thence to proceed to take part in operations against De Wet.

1ST SEPTEMBER.—The released prisoners passed by train en route to Belfast and Pretoria.

2ND.—No. 2660, Private R. Wells, 15th Hussars, attached, wounded whilst exercising horses. Open air church parade service, conducted by Colonel Clowes. The 1st Cavalry Brigade marched south to-day.

3RD.—Ordered to move to Welgelegan at 9 a.m. This was postponed until 11 a.m., but we did not move then. Mails arrived. Hear to-day that the cavalry brigade is to assemble at Carolina. I got in communication with a very high point some 20 miles away, and asked how General Buller was progressing on his march to Lydenburg, and was informed that he had just sent a message to the effect that he was heavily engaged, fronted with every kind of gun the Boers possessed, and for the present unable to move. " B " Squadron left on escort duty to Belfast.

4TH.—Marched at 9 a.m., and, after marching about four miles, overtook 1st Cavalry Brigade, who reported a party of snipers on left flank. We relieved the 1st Brigade flanking patrols, and they moved on, the 4th Cavalry Brigade following. Received information that General Ian Hamilton had come to the assistance of General Buller, and had enabled him to continue his march on Lydenburg.

No. 2851, Private L. Over, 15th Hussars, died at Bloemfontein of enteric fever.

5TH.—Marched at 6.30 a.m. Regiment escort to an ox convoy—a most tedious job. The party of snipers on the left flank still accompany the brigade. Passed over

SEPTEMBER, 1900.

a well and substantially made bridge, called "Groblers Burgh Bridge," near to which we halted for some time.

6TH.—As advance regiment we had a chance of disposing of the snipers to-day. They commenced as soon as we marched. "O" Battery was halted, and Colonel Clowes led a squadron towards a farm house, where the snipers had evidently assembled. The accurate firing of the battery was again noticeable when covering our advance. The first shell passed through an outhouse, the second went through the roof of same, and the third through the end wall of the farm house. That proved sufficient, the snipers cleared, and we were not again troubled with their attention. We then continued our march until we reached within about two miles of Carolina, where we bivouacked.

7TH.—The section of the outpost line, in command of Major Duff, "A" Squadron, attacked by Boers, who were easily repulsed. "B" Squadron re-joined. Colonel Mahon, whose brigade has arrived here, visited our camp.

8TH.—Same camp.

9TH.—The division, composed as follows, left Carolina at 5 a.m. to-day in a real South African mist, which is worse than rain. It was very cold. The following is the composition and organisation of the columns at present operating under Lieutenant-General French:—

DIVISIONAL STAFF.

A.D.C., Captain Sir J. Milbank, V.C.
A.D.C., Captain B. R. Fitzgerald.
C.S.O., Lieutenant-Colonel D. Haig.
D.A.A.G., Major Hon. C. E. Bingham.
D.A.A.G., Major A. G. Hunter Weston.
D.A.A.G., Major Foster.
D.A.A.G. for Intelligence, Captain J. Vaughan.
C.R.A., Colonel Eustace.
P.M.O., Lieutenant-Colonel Donovan.
M.O., Captain Buist.

September, 1900.

A.P.M., Captain Beech.
D.S.O., Captain Barry.
S.V.O., Captain Blenkinsop, D.S.O.

DIVISIONAL TROOPS.

French's Scouts.
Naval Detachments, with escort Argyll and Sutherland Highlanders. Captain Bearcroft, R.N.
Section 66th Battery, Royal Field Artillery.

1st Cavalry Brigade.
Bdr.-Gen. Gordon.
A.D.C., Capt. Wormald.
Bde.-Maj. Butter.
2nd Dragoons, 6th D. Gds.
6th Dragoons, " T " Batt. R.H.A.
" C " & " J " Sect. Pom-pom.
Sect. 1st Field Troop R.E.

4th Cavalry Brigade.
Maj.-Gen. Dickson, C.B.
A.D.C., Capt. Gage.
Bde.-Maj., Major Kenna, V.C.
7th D.G:, 8th Hussars.
14th Hussars, " O " Batt. R.H.A. (4 guns).
Sect. Pom-pom.
Sect. 1st Field Troop R.E.

Mahon's Brigade.
Bdr.-Gen. Mahon, D.S.O.
A.D.C., Prince Alexander of Teck.
Bde.-Maj., Capt. Bell Smythe.
18th Hussars (1 Sqdn.).
Imp. Light Horse, Lumsden's Horse.
N.Z.M. Rifles (3 Coys.).
Q. M. Inf. & Bushmen.
Imperial Yeomanry (1 Sqdn.).
3rd M. Inf. (3 Coys.).
" M " Batt. R.H.A.
2 Pom-poms, Yeomanry Field Hospital.

Infantry Brigade.
Lt.-Col. Spens.
A.D.C., Lieut. Bryant.
Bde.-Maj., Capt. Higgins.
2nd Shropshire L. Inf.
1st Suffolk Regt.

As the sun rose the mist cleared, and we came unexpectedly across a number of the enemy before leaving the high ground. Our guns came into action, and the enemy endeavoured to clear. To do so they had to ride from the position they occupied and had been surprised in, about 600 yards across the open, before they could get

SEPTEMBER, 1900.

out of sight over the next ridge. They effected an excellent retirement, dashing up the ridge in twos and threes. Despite this, however, we accounted for about 20 killed. Passing over the ground, a newly-dug grave was opened by our Field Troop, and found to contain a quantity of 12pdr. shells. Bivouacked at Klein Buffles Spruit.

10TH.—We are on the one job that no cavalryman can stand, *i.e.*, escort to an ox convoy. It seems to me that such an escort is always attended by a party of snipers on one or other of its flanks, who annoy one, and do little or no damage. Add to this a pace of about two miles per hour, a halt at mid-day for four hours, hilly country, and bad drifts, and you get about the sum total of the misery of a cavalry regiment escorting such a convoy. However, it was part of the work necessary to carry the war to a successful issue, and we had our crib and " stuck it." Bivouacked at 11.30 p.m. at Mount Ida.

11TH.—Sniped just before we left camp by a small party who came down amongst the high grass and mealie patch close to the edge of a river where our troops were washing prior to leaving camp. Total casualties from about 50 shots fired at about 1,000 yards—the officers' mess cart, 7th Dragoon Guards, struck! If the Boers are such expert marksmen, and cannot hit anyone in a brigade in camp, with no one replying to their fire, they must " bob " considerably. Bivouacked to-night about 10.30 p.m. at Hlomolom.

12TH.—Crossed the Komati River to-day, passed by Warmbath, and bivouacked at Onvervacht, at the foot of Nelspoort. The weather is getting much warmer.

13TH AND 14TH.— Remained in camp whilst the convoys of the two brigades were taken up the pass. So steep was the pass, that the wagons were off loaded and their contents carried up, and the teams had to be trebled before the wagons could be dragged to the top. The naval gun, part of the Divisional Force, with its limber,

SEPTEMBER, 1900.

required 52 and 48 oxen respectively to drag it up the steep ascent. The whole regiment, except half a squadron, was on outpost. General French reached Barberton, taking Landrost, releasing a number of our prisoners who had been sent to Barberton from Nootigedacht, and capturing £10,000 in gold and 53 locomotives.

15TH.—The troops ascended the pass and bivouacked about 1½ miles from its summit. We are at present on two-thirds rations, and horses on 7lbs. of corn per diem.

16TH.—Same camp. Rations 2½ biscuits, two-thirds rations of coffee, beef. Horses on 7lbs. corn per diem. Reconnaissance in the direction of the Moodie Goldfields.

17TH.—Captain Deare took out " C " Squadron, and about 200 Boers scooted on his approach. After being out several hours two prisoners were taken, other Boers getting clear away.

18TH.—No trace of the party of Boers could be seen to-day. Rained all night. Lieutenant Gilliatt, 16th Lancers, admitted to hospital suffering from enteric fever.

19TH.—Continued the march towards Barberton. Exceptionally hilly—mountainous we should have called it at home—journey. I am sure no convoy could have ascended the pass we came down. It was inches deep in dust in some parts, with huge boulders dotted here and there in others, the whole descent being exceedingly steep. It was with great difficulty that our convoys reached the bottom. The Boer convoys had taken this route, which was strewn with dozens of dead cattle. We bivouacked a short distance from the bottom of the pass.

20TH.—Crossed the Queen's River and camped about two miles from Barberton, which is a small town under the hills. Brevet-Colonel P. W. Le Gallais assumed command of General Hunter's troops.

21ST.—These pages are devoted to the records of the regiment solely, otherwise the next few pages could be easily filled with the " yarns "—" all on good authority "—that were circulated during the next few days about peace

SEPTEMBER, 1900.

rumours, our next trek, the end of the war, Reservists to go home, Cavalry Division for Pretoria, and many etcs. Officially, a summary of news from Lord Roberts declared:—" That there is now no longer a Boer force in existence, that what had been an organised army had destroyed their guns and separated, 700 crossing the border into Portuguese territory," and dubbing the remainder "A disorganised rabble." These few words undoubtedly described what the Boer force really was on this date.

23RD.—Lieutenant Gilliatt, 16th Lancers, died from enteric fever.

24TH.—The remains of Lieutenant Gilliatt buried at Barberton.

25TH TO 29TH.—We are in the same camp and enjoying a rest. Horses picking up under the good grazing afforded close to camp. Heard of General Pole Carew occupying Komati Poort and capturing a number of guns on the Selati River.

30TH.—In view of the mountainous district through which we were next to pass, Lieutenant Sir R. W. Levinge and the dismounted men proceeded by rail from Barberton to Machadodorp with the heavy baggage of the regiment.

1ST AND 2ND OCTOBER.—High winds and dust storms.

3RD.—Last night a fearful storm—no one other single adjective will describe it—commenced. It lightened, thundered, and hailed without ceasing throughout the night. Our blanket shelters were blown away, and we sat shivering on our saddles to await daybreak. For about half an hour, about 8 a.m., the storm abated, and we saddled up and commenced the march to Machadodorp. The commencement of the march was the signal for a fresh outburst from the elements, which repeated its performances of the previous night. We had proceeded a few miles without mishap, when suddenly a flash, more brilliant and longer than its predecessors, killed two men

OCTOBER, 1900.

and six horses of the Royal Horse Artillery. Many non-commissioned officers and men about these unfortunate comrades were stunned by the force of the shock. Late in the afternoon the storm ceased, and, plenty of wood being obtainable from a building close by, we soon had fires lighted and hot tea made to warm our bodies. The blankets and cloaks, pants and socks, were too wet to attempt to dry.

4TH.—Marched at 7 a.m. Food and forage issued after crossing the second drift on the way up the Devil's Kantoor. Continued the climb, but did not reach the top. The pass or road is not in bad condition, but it is very steep.

5TH.—Reached the summit after a five miles' pull and bivouacked. Grand view from the top of the Komati Valley, into which we commenced to descend on the 6th, and, reaching the railway station, Goodwan Siding, soon after crossing the river, which ran under the heights, we camped there. Supplies and a mail awaited us at the station.

7TH.—Followed the course of the River Komati again, and passed by Nooitgedacht, where the prisoners had been recently confined. Their camp had been surrounded by two barbed wire fences about four feet apart, the inner and outer standards (iron supports to the wire) being interlaced diagonally by strands of wire, which were also laced and twined about the inner and outer strands of wire—an effectual barrier. At intervals, and at a height of about 18ft. or 20ft., were placed electric installations. The little shelters made by the prisoners still remained. Shelters of bits of blankets, old clothing, mud, sacking, biscuit tins, and pieces of wood, in fact, anything, evidently that the unfortunate men could obtain to assist in protecting them from the severity of the weather. In the centre were two open tin sheds containing rude tables, on which the officers used to dine (sic).

Passing this interesting relic, we reached Water-

OCTOBER, 1900.

valonder, where we remained two hours, after which we ascended by a short but very steep hill on to the top of the plateau, near which we had first encamped on the 30th August, 1900. Here we met Lord Dundonald's Cavalry Brigade.

8TH.—Marched viâ Helvetia to Machadodorp. This time we camped on the east of the line—a much cleaner camp. We had not been in camp long before conversation with other regiments there, told us that the best part of the supposed good news we had heard at Barberton was quite wrong, and that things in general were not so rosy as we expected.

Brevet-Colonel B. T. Mahon, 8th Hussars, appointed to command of 12th Lancers.

9TH.—Commenced at once to re-horse and re-equip. I hope I may be pardoned for mentioning a personal incident. Since leaving Donker Hoek on the 24th April I have ridden the same horse daily without a change. By some means, after leaving Kameel Drift, the poor brute developed symptoms of skin disease, and soon after great bare patches, void of hair, were dotted about its body. These gradually spread. At Carolina I washed it well with diluted sheep dip, but that seemed to turn the bare patches of skin into hide, resembling that of a rhinoceros. After the Barberton trek it got no better, and to-day Major Wood sent me out of camp, and on my return I found he had had the poor brute destroyed out of humanity. I was much disappointed, but the poor brute could not have recovered. This now left us with about four or five horses only of the original lot with which we had first started.

Apart from this being an item of personal interest, I mention it to show what little time a horse would last. In six months only half-a-dozen were left out of our 450 with which we commenced—a casualty of three per diem.

To-day Major-General B. B. Dickson, C.B., who had

OCTOBER, 1900.

so far commanded the 4th Cavalry Brigade, issued a farewell address to all ranks of the regiment.

Farewell address of Major-General J. B. B. Dickson, C.B., commanding 4th Cavalry Brigade, on regiment leaving his brigade:—

"It is with great regret that I part with the 8th Hussars from my command. During the past seven months it has been frequently in action, and has invariably shown a true spirit of discipline and courage worthy of its traditions.

"Whether employed as contact squadrons, small patrols, or as part of the brigade, the officers, non-commissioned officers, and men have invariably displayed their soldierly qualities.

"Major-General Dickson begs to thank Colonel Clowes and all ranks under his command for the willing assistance they have always given him. He wishes them all success in the future."

10TH.—Brigadier-General Mahon's Brigade formed— 8th Hussars, 14th Hussars, 4 guns, "M" Battery, Royal Horse Artillery, Pom-Pom Section.

No. 5041, Private G. Pitchford, died in No. 4 General Hospital, Mooi River, of enteric fever.

12TH.—Marched via Dalmanutha to Geluk. On our way we came across 13 corpses of men, in all probability once part of General Buller's force, which we buried. We passed some splendidly-built trenches and earthworks, about which were considerable quantities of empty cartridge cases. Towards evening some skirmishing took place with a party of Boers to our front.

13TH.—Boers shelled the camp and outpost line at dawn. Almost immediately afterwards a very heavy rifle fire was opened on the outpost line, and all available troops were hurried into the trenches which had been made by General Buller's troops, during their advance on the Boer position at Dalmanutha on 27th and 28th August. The enemy's attack, which he pressed home with unusual courage and determination, presently

OCTOBER, 1900.
developed into an attempt to surround the brigade. This they almost succeeded in doing, a large force of Boers working round both flanks and a few appearing on the road leading back to Dalmanutha. This party was at once driven to a flank by the accurate fire of the pom-pom. Two picquets of "A" Squadron, under Lieutenant Wylam and Lieutenant Gilmour, 16th Lancers, attached, who were in a rather exposed position, suffered severely, all, with the exception of two men being killed, wounded or taken prisoners.

Lieutenant and Adjutant P. A. T. Jones was shot in the head early in the engagement, and died that night at Dalmanutha Station.

The brigade eventually made good its retirement towards Dalmanutha.

In this action Major Brown, 14th Hussars, gained his V.C.

REGIMENTAL CASUALTIES.

Killed: Lieutenant and Adjutant P. A. T. Jones, Lieutenant F. H. Wylam, No. 4413, Private F. Chubb, Private Langstone, No. 4263, Lance-Corporal C. J. Moore, 16th Lancers, and Private Bagnall, 16th Lancers, attached.

Wounded: Major C. E. Duff (slight), Second-Lieutenant Gilmour, 16th Lancers (attached), severe; No. 2178, Sergeant R. Tyler (severe); No. 3321, Private L. Reilly (severe); No. 3106, Private L. Kelly, and Private Leachs (severe); Private Holland, and Lance-Corporal Jackson, 16th Lancers, attached.

Missing: Private Gilbert (found on 15th inst. severely wounded).

Prisoners: Sergeant Rawley, Corporal Pye, Lance-Corporals Greenwood and Bowes, Privates Crow, Bryne, and Holland (wounded), Lance-Corporal Jackson, 16th Lancers (wounded), Scott, Headley, Greer, Patterson, Murray, Mortham, Reilly (wounded), Leach (wounded).

OCTOBER, 1900.

The 14th Hussars, "M" Battery, and the Pom-Pom Section also lost heavily. Captain Taylor, in command of the latter, was killed.

14TH.—Saddled at dawn. A reconnaissance to-day showed the enemy to be still holding the same positions. No engagement took place. The enemy's gun was placed on almost the same spot we occupied at Geluk on the 21st August, 1900.

No. 2733, Private J. Thorogood, 3rd Hussars, attached, died at Helpmakaar from concussion of the brain.

15TH.—Reveillé 3.30 a.m. Marched at dawn. The enemy had retired, and we passed over the scene of the engagement on 13th. By the bank of the stream we found Private Gilbert. He had been severely wounded by an explosive bullet. The Boers had carried him down to the stream that he might be near the water, but they left him there without food or blankets. The poor fellow must have had two miserable days and nights, especially so as it rained during the whole night on the 13th and 14th. It is a pleasure to know that he afterwards recovered. Bivouacked at Twyflaar.

16TH.—Marched to Roodebloom. Late in the day firing was heard. It transpired afterwards that the 1st Brigade had been attacked by a large force of the enemy who had recovered from a "disorganised rabble," and were once more in the field as an organised enemy.

The 1st, 4th, and General Mahon's Brigades were now separated, but were to a certain extent all moving parallel. During the night almost all the horses in the regiment stampeded, but were subsequently recovered.

17TH.—Reveillé 3.30. Stood to for some time in case of an attack. During to-day's march we passed over Klipheuvil, the highest point in the Transvaal. Shortly after reaching our camp at Sterkfontein we heard firing in the direction of General Gordon's Brigade. The enemy had attacked the brigade as the outpost line was being thrown out. They were repulsed. Close to this

SOUTH AFRICAN WAR

OCTOBER, 1900.

camp is the source of the Vaal. The nearest town—Ermelo.

18TH.—Reveillé 3.30 a.m. Stood to. Moved towards Spitz Kop, which was held by the enemy. Camped late at night in a very bad place for wood and water. The enemy have been reinforced, and are now strong enough to hamper the movements of each of the three brigades. Shortly after camping, *i.e.*, as soon as we had succeeded in finding a little wood and water, and had partaken of a frugal—very frugal—meal, the word was passed round that all fires were to be extinguished, and that all ranks were to be prepared to saddle at a moment's notice.

19TH.—Reveillé 3 a.m. Another day similar to the last. Passed by Spit Kop. Our brigade was on the right, and the 1st Brigade in the centre. The latter was again engaged to-day by the enemy, who had a gun on the kop. We halted for about two hours at mid-day. A patrol of "A" Squadron, under Sergeant Leopold, had a narrow shave to-day, the enemy almost succeeding in getting the patrol into a space surrounded by wire. It was necessary to turn a gun on the enemy before they would be persuaded to retire.

20TH.—Reveillé 3 a.m. It is, of course, dark at that hour. On rising, there is as little noise made in camp as possible. As soon as the horses are saddled, the outposts are considerably strengthened, and a gun is sent out in addition, so that, should the camp be attacked at dawn we should be prepared. A patrol of "C" Squadron was captured by the enemy to-day whilst examining a farm for Boers. After stripping the men of all they had the enemy allowed them to re-join the regiment. Marched as far as Bethel and camped.

21ST.—Remained in camp. The outpost in touch with enemy all day. During the morning several men in khaki came towards the outpost line held by the Carabiniers. Making signs that they wished to speak with them, the sergeant in command went out to meet one, who advanced

OCTOBER, 1900.

in front of the others. When almost close to the man the sergeant was shot down and instantly killed. Our camp was amongst some very dry grass, and to-day this caught fire, and, fanned by a strong wind, swept towards "A" Squadron lines. The horses were let loose just in time, but kits, etc., were destroyed, and the convoy had a narrow escape, one portion being slightly burned.

General French visited the camp, and ordered a parade of the regiment. In a brief speech "he thanked the regiment for its past services, and expressed his belief that, if called upon for further efforts, the appeal would be cheerfully answered."

22ND.—Reveillé 2 a.m. Outpost line again strengthened. Very wet. Enemy on flanks and rear. The Carabiniers' outposts were attacked near a kraal as the brigades moved out of camp, but they were more than well prepared, and inflicted very heavy losses on the enemy. As we passed beyond Bethel the enemy came in and occupied the town again.

During the afternoon a fearful hailstorm came on, and at the same time a party of the enemy appeared in front of us. The wind blew from the front, and it was impossible to get the horses to face the fury of the storm. The thunder and lightning was almost as powerful and heavy as the Barberton storm, two Kaffirs and two horses being killed by the lightning. As the storm spent itself we advanced a short distance, and succeeded in driving off the enemy for a time.

23RD.—Reveillé 2.45 a.m. Enemy followed all day. Our progress is very slow owing to our oxen in the convoy being done up. Rained all day. Bivouacked at Windehoek.

24TH.—Reveillé 2.30 a.m. Continued our march. The enemy are said to have been joined to-day by a Heidleberg command. Bivouacked Kaffir Kuil.

25TH.—Reveillé 2.30 a.m. Continued our march.

OCTOBER, 1900.
Less sniping to-day than on any day previously. Bivouacked Witkop.

26TH.—Reveillé 2.30 a.m. Passed Nigel Gold Mines, where our troops had a fort—about 9½ miles from Heidleberg. The fort is very strongly held—wire entanglements stretching all round. It needs to be, too, considering the distance from the town and the number of Boers about. Rain. Arrived at Heidleberg, where two mails awaited us.

This march was the most trying time the regiment has experienced in South Africa. There was continual sniping and slight attacks on the flank and rear throughout the march. The entire regiment was on outpost duty night after night, men in many cases being on sentry as often as five consecutive nights. The weather during the latter part of the march was as bad as it could be, and owing to the early starts and late hours of arrival in bivouac men suffered greatly from exposure and lack of food.

27TH.—Same camp. Another mail arrived. Each non-commissioned officer and man issued with one pint of beer. Very heavy rains. To-day we had the best issue of beef rations that we ever had. It was frozen, but of excellent quality.

Lieutenant F. M. Jennings re-joined regiment after escorting Boer prisoners to Ceylon.

28TH.—Same camp.

29TH.—The 16th Lancers attached left by rail to re-join their regiment. They had done very good work, and were a fine lot of men, and were deservedly popular with all ranks of the 8th Hussars. Colonel Clowes thanked them on parade for their services, and they left amid many hearty cheers from all.

30TH.—Left for Pretoria, viâ Springs, where we arrived towards evening.

31ST.—Lord Roberts inspected the Cavalry Division.

OCTOBER, 1900.

Extract from the "London Gazette," dated October, 1900:—

8th King's Royal Irish Hussars.

To be Companion of the Distinguished Service Order—Captain Robert Lambert.

To be Lieutenant-Colonel (half pay)—Major D. E. Wood.

To be Brevet Lieutenant-Colonel—Major C. E. Duff.

To have the Distinguished Conduct Medal—Sergeant-Major W. Mountford, No. 2933, Squadron-Sergeant-Major J. F. Burns, No. 3714, Sergeant E. Parry.

The undermentioned were "mentioned in despatches"—Squadron-Sergeant-Major F. Stretch, Squadron-Sergeant-Major S. J. Spain, No. 3782, Sergeant J. W. Morton, and Private Hannigan.

1ST NOVEMBER.—Continued our march. It has seemed quite strange to-day to march without hearing the sound of the Mauser, and without patrols being hurried out to drive off any particularly troublesome party. Rain.

2ND.—Rained almost all last night and all day to-day; what condition we should be in without the cavalry cloak I don't know. No matter how it rains, our bodies are kept almost quite dry, but our pants, putties, and boots are soaked.

3RD.—Marched through Bapsfontein and bivouacked at Reitvlei. Rain continued until about an hour before we entered Pretoria, passing under Klapper Kop Fort. We marched through the town, and camped about half a mile beyond the old racecourse.

4TH.—Lieutenant C. E. Soames and Lieutenant R. W. Allen joined the regiment with the following draft, having landed at Port Elizabeth on 23rd August.

Draft of 2 officers, 2 corporals, and 63 privates arrived at Port Elizabeth, per s.s. "Winkfield." Draft consisted of:—

SOUTH AFRICAN WAR

NOVEMBER, 1900.

Sec.-Lieut. C. E. Soames.
Sec.-Lieut. R. W. Allen.
3145 15th Hrs., Cpl. W. Parrott.
3146 15th Hrs., Cpl. Parrott.
3320 Lce.-Cpl. C. Wilkins.
4427 Pte. H. Anderson.
2811 15th Hrs., Pte. W. Beton.
4519 Pte. P. Byrne.
4632 Pte. J. Hazeltine.
2912 15th Hrs., Pte. W. Hutchins.
4529 Pte. J. Varley.
4476 Pte. R. Lambert.
2728 15th Hrs., Pte. R. Mears.
3292 Pte. H. McCann.
4638 Pte. F. Nicholson.
4395 Pte. H. Summerfield.
4357 Lce.-Cpl. W. Pocklington.
4631 Pte. W. Collard.
4601 Pte. L. Gaisford.
4321 Pte. F. Hunt.
4274 Pte. J. Ledwidge.
2733 15th Hrs., Pte. R. Luxton.
2928 15thHrs., Pte. W. Morris.
4380 Pte. E. Street.
4481 Pte. A. Jeffries.
4592 Pte. M. White.
4434 Pte. F. Wright.
4367 Pte. T. Anson.
4468 Pte. Allen.
4599 Pte. Delahaye.
4502 Pte. Holohan.
4623 Pte. Knight.
4385 Pte. Manders.

4288 Pte. Plant.
4619 Pte. Mack.
4633 Pte. Boston.
4440 Pte. Holohan.
3426 Pte. Lacey.
4454 Pte. Myerscough.
4630 Pte. Robinson.
4414 Pte. Smith.
2858 15th Hussars, Lce.-Cpl. Murphy.
4586 Pte. Bennett.
4637 Pte. Woodbridge.
4442 Pte. Brennan.
4384 Pte. Eccles.
4621 Pte. Farmer.
4353 Pte. Haynes.
4447 Pte. Powell.
4322 Pte. Rice.
4435 Pte. Robinson.
4240 Pte. Royle.
2678 15th Hussars, Pte. Short.
4583 Pte. Jenkins.
4276 Pte. Mulligan.
4625 Pte. Smith.
4094 Pte. Kayes.
4582 Pte. Hare.
2881 15th Hrs., Pte. Thompson.
4130 Pte. Goodison.
4335 Pte. Neal.
2667 15th Hussars, Pte. Latter.
4464 Pte. Savage.
2577 15th Hussars, Pte. Stewart.
3063 15th Hrs., Lce.-Cpl. Chart.

The undermentioned non-commissioned officers and men, Reservists, 4th Hussars, posted to regiment:—

2881 Sq.-Sgt.-Maj. T. Williams.
2595 Cpl. L. Howe.
2662 Cpl. Clements.
2926 Cpl. Green.
2678 Cpl. W. Neal.
2868 Lce.-Cpl. O. Neal.

2656 Lce.-Cpl. Tilbie.
2645 Lce.-Cpl. Winterflood.
2897 Lce.-Cpl. Gerlack.
2774 Lce.-Cpl. Ellis.
2709 Pte. T. Hook.
2726 Pte. G. Hill.

5TH.—Colonel P. W. J. Le Gallais, 8th Hussars, killed in action at Bothaville, when by the greatest dash he had

NOVEMBER, 1900.

just given Commandant De Wet the first severe defeat that General had sustained. General Mahon appointed Governor of Kordofan, Egypt, and relieved of his command.

"O" Battery, Royal Horse Artillery, 7th Dragoon Guards, 8th Hussars, and 14th Hussars, again formed the 4th Cavalry Brigade.

Commenced to re-equip, and continued to do so daily. Issued with tents—the first we have slept in since 20th April, 1900.

6TH.—Major-General Dickson, C.B., being about to return home, published the following in Brigade Orders:
"As Major-General Dickson is about to proceed to England, he cannot leave the brigade, who have fought so valiantly and successfully, without saying 'good-bye.' He tenders his thanks to his Staff for their untiring energy, and to the officers, non-commissioned officers, and men of "O" Battery, Royal Horse Artillery, and the three regiments for their discipline, determination, and valour. He wishes them a safe return to their homes at an early date."

7TH.—Major-General Dickson left for England.

10TH.—Extract from Divisional Orders:—
Farewell Order.

" The Cavalry Division, having for a time broken up
" into brigade units, the Lieutenant-General, on relin-
" quishing the command, desires to express his deep regret
" in severing his immediate connection with the splendid
" force it has been his honour and privilege to command,
" throughout an almost continuous series of engagements,
" and active operations, commencing February last to the
" present time. General French recalls with pride and
" satisfaction, the many occasions during the period upon
" which he has personally witnessed the intrepid gallantry
" displayed by all ranks of the Cavalry Division, a
" glorious reminiscence which will be ever present to the
" end of his life.

NOVEMBER, 1900.

" His warmest thanks are due to the brigadiers, com-
" manding officers, squadron commanders, officers, non-
" commissioned officers, and men for the skill, courage,
" and endurance which has been mainly instrumental in
" securing the successful results attained."

11TH.—Lieutenant R. Lambert appointed adjutant, vice Lieutenant P. A. T. Jones, died of wounds received in action.

15TH.—No. 4306, Private W. Fawcett, died at Pretoria of enteric fever.

19TH.—Marched from Pretoria and bivouacked at Reitfontein, en route to Rustenberg to join the 2nd Cavalry Brigade.

20TH.—Continued march and bivouacked at Wolhuters Kop. Tremendous thunderstorm at night.

21ST.—Bivouacked at Buffles Poort, near Sterkstroom. During to-day's march heavy firing was heard on the south side of the Magaliesburg as we passed under the north side. Considerable difficulty with the transport owing to heavy roads.

22ND.—Arrived at Rustenburg and joined General Broadwood's Column. The other regiments—10th Hussars and 12th Lancers—expressed their pleasure in having one of the celebrated French's cavalry regiments brigaded with them, and plied us with all sort of questions as to our latest doings. "Q" Battery, Royal Horse Artillery, an Elswick gun, and a pom-pom completed the brigade.

23RD.—No. 4439, Shoeing-Smith Brophy, re-joined from Mounted Infantry.

24TH.—Left Rustenberg to proceed against General Delarey, who is reported about 20 miles away on the south side of the Magaliesberg. Marched through Magato Pass and afterwards through a bush-veldt country before bivouacking at Tweerivier.

25TH.—Similar kind of country. Bivouacked at Hartebeestfontein.

NOVEMBER, 1900.

26TH.—Returned to Rustenberg in one day's march. It afterwards transpired that General Delarey had tapped our telegraph cable wire behind us and recalled the brigade; the message reading as if sent from Pretoria by Lord Kitchener.

29TH.—Again left Rustenberg, proceeding in the same direction, and camping at Tweerivier.

30TH.—Marched to Kosterfontein. Our left flank met with some slight opposition, which was repulsed by the 10th Hussars, the advanced regiment to-day. For the information of any who are not aware of the fact, I may here mention that in a cavalry brigade each regiment takes its turn in finding the various advanced and rear guards and escorts to the guns and convoy.

1ST DECEMBER.—The brigade did not move, but our squadrons reconnoitred and operated in and about the Kosterfontein Valley, destroying considerable quantities of supplies. During the day the enemy attacked the picquets of the 12th Lancers, and took some of them prisoners, and later in the day they drove in a picquet of the 10th Hussars. Our squadrons on their return occupied the outpost line from which the picquets had been driven.

2ND.—An early move was made in a south-east direction towards Vlakfontein on the high veldt.

An important point—or perhaps I may say two important points—have been noted by us since joining the 2nd Cavalry Brigade. One, which I think I may say we learned, and one which we taught, viz.: First, that the advance guard should ride in pairs; and the second that the advance guard should be considerably further in advance than had apparently been the custom in the 2nd Cavalry Brigade. The enemy attacked the outpost line again to-day.

3RD.—Marched at daybreak towards Olifants Nek in the Magaliesberg. After proceeding about three miles the enemy were met with, and an engagement commenced

SOUTH AFRICAN WAR

DECEMBER, 1900.

and lasted until well into the afternoon. The regiment was chiefly engaged on the left flank and left front of the brigade. "C" Squadron were very hotly pressed at one time, Captain Burns Lindow, No. 2868, Lance-Corporal Neale, 4th Hussars, No. 3671, Private Maher, and No. 4476, Private Lambert, being wounded before "B" Squadron galloped up and strengthened them. The Elswick gun was very useful to-day. This gun is of a very heavy type, and its weight told greatly against its mobility. It was manned by men from the Elswick Factory—Volunteers.

The enemy was gradually driven back, and on nearing the nek information was received of the disaster near Buffles Poort to the convoy proceeding from Pretoria to Rustenberg laden with supplies. On reaching the nek the brigade off-saddled for one hour, and then proceeded towards Buffles Poort, close to which we bivouacked at midnight. The horses had been under saddle for 20 hours, with the exception of the one hour from about 5 to 6 p.m. No water in the bivouac.

4TH.—Moved off at daybreak and crossed the Sterkstroom below Buffles Poort. We found that the first half of the convoy, which was moving in two divisions, had been captured, 40 wagons being taken by the Boers, who burned the remainder, and took about 100 men of the escort prisoners.

The guns and mails had been saved by great personal bravery of the gunners, who finally dragged their guns away after firing several rounds of case shot.

The wagons and contents were still burning, and a large number of the oxen, with which the wagons had been spanned, were lying dead by the road. Bivouacked near Sterkwater.

5TH.—Marched back towards Rustenburg. Bivouacked at Oorzak, near Kroondal.

6TH.—Orders received to march back to Rustenburg, but they were countermanded, and we remained in camp.

DECEMBER, 1900.

From various sources information had been received that there is a very large force of Boers within a radius of a very few miles.

7TH.—Moved a short distance, and camped in Kroomriver Valley, commonly called the "Happy Valley" by the inhabitants. In this valley, which nestles amid the Magaliesberg, large quantities of food stuffs were found in the farm houses and grounds. A portion of General Clements' force occupied the range on the south side.

8TH, 9TH, AND 10TH.—Remained in camp. Each morning the troops were fully prepared to move at the shortest notice, but we remained until the 11th, when we moved back to bivouac at Oorzak.

12TH.—Remained in camp.

13TH.—In the early morning heavy gun firing was heard in the direction of General Clements' camp, but no communication could be established by helio as there was no sun. At mid-day the brigade moved out of bivouac, crossed the Sterkstroom, and halted at Elandskraal. Soon after arriving we heard that General Clements had been driven off the Magaliesberg with heavy losses, and that every precaution was to be taken in case our weak brigade should be attacked. The convoy, which we had left at our last bivouac, was sent for, and arrived very late. Very strong outposts thrown out.

14TH.—Reveillé 2.30 a.m. Marched back at daybreak to Oorzak, and after halting three hours marched into Rustenberg, where we remained until the 20th.

20TH.—Marched to Waterkloof, near Olifants Nek, about 3 p.m.

21ST.—Reveillé 2 a.m. Marched to the top of the pass leading into the "Happy Valley," and returned to Oorzak in afternoon.

22ND.—Remained in bivouac.

23RD.—Reveillé 1.30 a.m. Marched at 3 a.m. through Olifants Nek in a south-east direction, meeting with considerable opposition; Schoenkloof.

SOUTH AFRICAN WAR

DECEMBER, 1900.

No. 3087, Corporal F. Pye, 15th Hussars, severely wounded; No. 3574, Private C. O'Connor, and No. 4332, Private J. Grant, wounded.

24TH.—Reveillé 2.30 a.m. Marched eastwards and bivouacked late at night—Christmas Eve—at Welverdiend, on the Johannesburg and Klerksdorp Railway, where General Gordon's Brigade was in bivouac.

25TH.—Christmas Day. Remained in camp. Colonel Gordon's Brigade left.

26TH.—Colonel C. E. Knox assumed command of the 2nd Cavalry Brigade.

27TH.—Marched from Welverdiend towards Ventersdorp. The columns operating together now are Colonel Gordon's, Generals Babington's and Kekewick's, and Colonel Knox's. The whole were under command of General French, who marched with our brigade. The country over which we travelled bore unmistakable traces of the enemy having recently left. Bivouacked at Kaffir Kaal.

28TH.—Reached Ventersdorp, where we found six other columns.

29TH.—Marched towards Potchefstroom in heavy rain.

30TH.—Arrived at Potchefstroom with about 15,000 sheep and 9,000 cattle.

1ST JANUARY, 1901.—Regiment turned out at 4 a.m. to reconnoitre towards the Vaal and to secure the safety of an observation post near there. Found no trace of enemy, and returned to camp.

2ND.—No. 4017, Lance-Corporal P. Marshall died at Rustenberg of dysentery.

3RD.—" C " Squadron entrained for Germiston (Johannesburg).

4TH.—Remainder of regiment entrained for same town and bivouacked close to the station.

5TH.—Marched about three miles to Bezindenhout. Camped near a remount depôt there, about $1\frac{1}{2}$ miles from Johannesburg.

JANUARY, 1901.

No. 3799, Private W. Thompson, died at Pretoria of enteric fever.

6TH.—Lieutenant C. M. Threlfall and Second-Lieutenant E. G. Warner joined regimental headquarters from England.

No. 3923, Private J. Gill, died at Rustenberg of enteric fever.

7TH.—Four of us visited Johannesburg, and before returning had a tea, consisting only of tea, bread and butter, and eggs, for which we were charged 13s.

8TH.—Equipment and stores drawn and issued.

9TH.—The brigade moved out at 5 a.m. and conducted a reconnaissance in the direction of Krugersdorp. No enemy were seen. Brigade returned to camp at 7.30 p.m.

12TH.—Early this morning guns were heard a short distance away. Quite surprised of course, everyone prepared for a move, and before one could quite realise what was happening the brigade was out of camp and on its way to two railway stations on the Johannesburg-Pretoria line—Kaalfontein and Zuurfontein—both of which had been attacked. Unhampered by any convoy, we were soon on the spot, but found that the stations had successfully resisted the attacks with but little loss. We followed the enemy, and found he still held the next ridge. General Baden-Powell, who, with his troopers of the South African Constabulary, was co-operating, returned at once, otherwise a big bag might have been made, as the enemy, about 1,500 strong, were not five miles away, with his convoy outspanned. Needless to say, as soon as we appeared over the ridge we received immediate attention, a pom-pom and rifle fire greeting us. No. 4034, Corporal J. Conroy, was dangerously wounded on the first ridge, and on reaching the second, No. 3285, Corporal J. Garrett, was wounded in the leg. These were the only regimental casualties. The Boers scooted off across the large open plain, assisted by our guns, which, owing to the open

JANUARY, 1901.

nature of their retirement, had but little chance of doing much damage.

I had a chance of looking round Kaalfontein Station afterwards, and found the sheds and buildings riddled with bullet holes. The slight losses suffered by the defenders were easily accounted for when one viewed their admirable wire entanglements round the station, and their shelter trenches, which were deep enough for a man to stand upright in without being seen. These were all tunnelled, to allow any one part, severely pressed, to be reinforced from another without exposure. The enemy must have lost heavily, as they came so close that dead horses were found on the borders of the wire, and a Boer Commandant, mortally wounded, was found on its outskirts, as well as several others too badly wounded to be carried away by their comrades.

We bivouacked near the station. Owing to our hurried departure from camp, the troops had turned out without food, except what they chanced to have in their haversacks. Consequently the great majority had nothing until the convoy arrived, on the 13th, on which day we had reveillé at 3.15 a.m., to be ready should the enemy return.

14TH.—1st Brigade arrived and camped close to us.

15TH.—Corporal Conroy died of wounds received on 12th inst. Captain Greathed, Lieutenant Lomer, and C.V.S. Wadsworth, with the details, left behind at Rustenberg (most of whom had been sick), re-joined.

21ST.—First notification received in camp that our beloved Queen is in a precarious state of health.

Three troops of "B" Squadron went to Irene and one to Zuurfontein Station.

23RD.—Turned out at dawn. General French suspected that an attack would be made on Johannesburg. After reconnoitring some distance the brigade returned to camp, on reaching which we heard of the sad death of the Queen. A subdued tone seemed to at once prevail, and all ranks felt the loss of Her Majesty deeply.

JANUARY, 1901.

Second-Lieutenant H. C. Malet joined on appointment from Cape Mounted Rifles.

24TH.—Preparations are being made for a trek. Stores, etc., have been drawn up and issued.

27TH.—Marched at 8 a.m. to commence what is now (after the war) known as the Eastern Trek—a wide, sweeping movement by   columns, commanded by   all treking east in the order named, commencing from the south and ending with   column, which started from Belfast. Bivouacked at Bapsfontein.

28TH.—Marched at 7 a.m. For the present operations orders were issued to-day that all produce the troops come across is either to be brought on by the brigade or destroyed. Bivouacked at Blesboklaagte.

29TH.—Colonel Allenby's column, on our right, had a brush with the enemy, who afterwards came in contact with our brigade. Their convoy could be seen in the distance, but too far away to chase. The Elswick gun made excellent practice to-day. Bivouacked at Steinkoolspruit.

30TH.—Did not move camp.

31ST.—The regiment left camp before the brigade, and conducted a reconnaissance in the direction of to-morrow's intended line of march towards Springboklaagte. "A" Squadron came in touch with the enemy and captured about 100 head of their cattle.

1ST FEBRUARY.—Reveillé 3 a.m. The regiment covered a wide extent of front on the right of the brigade, and encountered the enemy early. A running fight ensued, and lasted all day, the enemy being successfully driven from ridge to ridge. Late in the afternoon they occupied a farm, round which a lot of firing took place. No. 3739, Private S. Scott, No. 3090, Private Cotton, 15th Hussars, and No. 3568, Private Tait, were afterwards found to be missing. The former was never seen afterwards, and from subsequent reports received it was substantially

FEBRUARY, 1901.
proved that he was killed and buried by the Boers. The two latter afterwards re-joined. Bivouacked at Haasfontein late at night, after a long and tiring day.

2ND.—Reveillé 3.30 a.m. Continued the running fight, and bivouacked at Witbank.

3RD.—Reveillé 5.30 a.m. Moved at 2 p.m. a short distance, and bivouacked at Yzarkfontein.

4TH.—Reveillé 3 a.m. Marched at 5 a.m., and bivouacked at Eerstegeluk, south-east of Bethel.

5TH.—Reveillé 3 a.m. To-day we passed over part of the same ground as on our march from Machadodorp, and at the same farm, where the men of " C " Squadron were then taken prisoners, we had No. 2897, Lance-Corporal Gerlach, 4th Hussars, and No. 4305, Private McKay, wounded. The latter was wonderfully lucky, as the bullet passed through the helmet and grazed the scalp of the head—a lucky escape. Bivouacked at the farm—Middleplaats. This farm, occupied by Mrs. Van Dyk, who had thus twice led our men on by asserting that none of the enemy were about, was destroyed on leaving on the 6th, when we rose at 3 a.m. During the day we passed Spit Kop and Swartz Kop, and the brigades secured all the roads leading into and from Ermelo, in the hope of finding the enemy were holding the town. They were found to have cleared, however, and we camped about two miles from the town, near Bushmans Tafel Kop, during heavy rains.

No. 4447, Private F. Powell, died of enteric fever at Johannesburg.

7TH.—Marched about nine miles east of Ermelo to Mooi Plaats, and bivouacked to await supplies.

8TH.—Boer outposts to be plainly seen on the ridge close to camp.

9TH.—" B " Squadron left for Ermelo to bring supplies. A picquet of " C " Squadron was attacked, but succeeded in repulsing the enemy.

10TH.—Sunday evening church service well attended.

FEBRUARY, 1901.

12TH.—Moved out in a heavy mist and bivouacked at Vaalbank.

13TH.—With "C" Squadron as escort, I was sent out to find General Alderson and send an important helio cypher message from General French.

14TH.—Reveillé 3.30 a.m. Marched over some boggy country and bivouacked at Driepan.

15TH.—Reveillé 3.30 a.m. Similar kind of country. Bivouacked at Idalia.

16TH.—Reached Piet Retief with but slight opposition. Boers had passed through the town only a few hours before. Several surrenders, including the Llandrost.

The regiment, with a section of "Q" Battery, occupied a ridge about two miles north-east of the town, where we remained until 15th March, 1901. Three-quarter rations to-day for both man and horse.

17TH.—Scale of rations reduced to two-thirds.

18TH.—Half rations.

Second-Lieutenant H. M. FitzHerbert and following draft, composed as under, sailed from home for South Africa, and disembarked 18th March, 1901, ex. s.s. "Columbia":—

Sec.-Lieut. H. N. M. Fitz-Herbert		4596 Pte. Fairbrother.	
2680	15th Hrs., Sgt. E. Lewis.	4127 Pte. Frain.	
3306	15th Hrs., Cpl. Allan.	4679 Pte. W. Fitzgerald.	
4452	Pte. W. Barnes.	4493 Pte. Googan.	
4176	Pte. W. Bell.	3433 Cpl. Goulder.	
3715	Pte. J. Binns.	4451 Pte. Harris.	
4795	Pte. G. Brien.	4814 Pte. Hubbard.	
4432	Pte. E. Caney.	4673 Pte. Hughes.	
4674	Pte. E. Cavan.	4230 Pte. W. Johnstone.	
4487	Pte. W. Carr.	4505 Pte. Kelbrick.	
4290	Pte. Carroll.	4235 Pte. King.	
4608	Pte. Cousins.	4015 Pte. Lambert.	
4173	Pte. Daily.	4744 Pte. McDonald.	
4524	Pte. T. Dollard.	4171 Pte. McEvoy.	
4061	Pte. Donlon.	4788 Pte. McGowan.	
3618	Pte. Donnelly.	4826 Pte. McManus.	
4742	Pte. Doyle.	4756 Pte. J. Mills.	
		4689 Pte. W. Moore.	

FEBRUARY, 1901.

4150 Pte. McCarthy.	4186 Pte. Shea.
4349 Pte. Mulhall.	4208 Pte. J. Spencer.
4823 Pte. Murdock.	4107 Pte. W. Tait.
4525 Pte. Parr.	4562 Pte. Thompson.
4226 Pte. Page.	4179 Pte. Ward.
4509 Pte. G. Patton.	4733 Pte. G. Walton.
4103 Pte. Payne.	4748 Pte. Walker.
4508 Pte. J. Porter.	3665 Pte. Weir.
4804 Pte. W. Prentice.	4280 Pte. Wells.
4423 Pte. W. Raban.	4683 Pte. G. Wilson.
4283 Pte. Reilly.	4695 Pte. H. Woan.
5117 Pte. G. Salter.	

19TH.—Rained all day. Horses on 4lbs. corn. Troops on half rations.

20TH.—Men on quarter rations, viz., $1\frac{1}{4}$ biscuits, a little coffee, no sugar, plenty of mutton, but no salt. Enemy attacked outposts. The wet weather continues. A general drizzle prevails during the day, and very often turns into heavy rains at night. A convoy has left Utrecht with supplies, but is stopped by swollen drifts. There are five brigades here, so that an enormous convoy would be required to keep us on full rations. There are any amount of rumours as to what is happening elsewhere, but these mostly turned out to be the customary "yarns."

21ST.—No more biscuit ration or coffee. To-day 2ozs. rice and $\frac{1}{4}$lb. jam and some mealie had to suffice. Horses 2lbs. corn. Rained day and night.

22ND.—Continued raining. For general information it was published in Brigade Orders of the 20th that the convoys trying to reach us had an impossible task at present, as the rivers Pongola and Intombi, 50 yards and 200 yards wide respectively, were not spanned by bridges, and had to be forded. This was impossible in their present state of flood. General French rightly termed these present conditions as "a most unfortunate state of affairs."

Rations to-day $\frac{1}{2}$lb. mealie, with plenty of meat, but no salt.

23RD.—Rain ceased at noon. Advantage was taken of

FEBRUARY, 1901.

this to move camp higher up the ridge. Rations ½lb. mealie.

24TH.—A drizzle this morning. Kaffirs have informed the authorities that Boer guns are buried close at hand. Digging operations commenced. These were partly successful, as the small parts of big guns were found carefully greased and wrapped in canvas. The smallest parts being placed in boxes.

Two gallant fellows of the Scots Guards were drowned to-day whilst endeavouring to get a rope across the swollen drift in the hope that it would then be possible to devise means of hauling supplies over. Rations ½lb. mealie, meat, no salt. Horses no corn. I have omitted to state that the horses are taken out daily to graze.

25TH.—To-day General French expressed in Divisional Orders " How highly he appreciated the spirit and bearing of the troops under the privations they were suffering from bad weather and short food," and directed officers commanding units to let the troops know this.

Results of the operations during this Eastern Trek were published:—

Boers killed, wounded, or captured	392
Surrendered	353
Total Boers accounted for	745
Cannon taken, including a Maxim	7
Rifles	606
Rounds of ammunition	161,630
Horses and mules	6,504
Trek oxen	4,362
Other cattle	20,986
Sheep	158,130
Wagons and carts	1,604
Mealies and oat hay	4,000,000lbs.

Rations ½lb. mealie.

26TH.—Rained ceased.

27TH.—A substitute for coffee has been tried, viz., burnt mealie; not at all nice, especially as we have no sugar.

SOUTH AFRICAN WAR 83

FEBRUARY, 1901.
" C " Squadron returned from escorting a small convoy in. They walked dismounted as much as they could. Some of the horses were too weak to walk into camp on returning.

28TH.— General Kitchener complimented General French and his troops on their work and behaviour, and on the difficulties they had overcome.

1ST MARCH.—8lbs. oats were issued for the horses to-day, and the poor beasts well deserved some food, as the grazing was about done.

Captain Page re-joined, and Second-Lieutenant Hon. R. N. D. Ryder joined from Staffordshire Militia. Colonel Alderson's Brigade arrived.

2ND.—Half rations issued, viz., 2½ biscuits, 1oz. sugar, 2ozs. cheese, mealie, meal, coffee, meat.

Private Tait, reported missing on 1st, re-joined.

Extract from London Gazette:—" Lieutenant R. Lambert, adjutant, to be captain, to complete establishment, ante-dated to October 13th, 1900.

3RD.—Half rations. One Howitzer and two Creusot 12-pdrs. dug up out of very wet ground about four miles away from the place where the limbers belonging to same were found.

Captain Viscount Garnock and the following draft of 200 non-commissioned officers and men landed from s.s. " Idaho " at Durban, and proceeded to Volksrust, where they remained to do duty in that district pending arrival of regiment.

Draft, composed as under, embarked at Queenstown 3rd March, 1901, and sailed from home for South Africa, and disembarked 1st April, 1901, ex. s.s. " Idaho " :—

Capt. R. Viscount Garnock.	2956 Lce.-Cpl. Burnside.
1883 15th Hrs., Staff-Sgt. Farr.	3719 Cpl. Lewis.
Rogers.	5270 Lce.-Cpl. Fairclough.
2355 Sgt. Mellish.	4600 Lce.-Cpl. Pilling.
2726 15th Hrs., Sgt. Sharkey.	3312 Tptr. Morris.
3756 Sgt. Kershaw.	3316 Tptr. Proctor.
4250 Cpl. Challinor.	3884 S.S Billaine.

84 DIARY OF THE

MARCH, 1901.

4690 Pte. Armour.
4802 Pte. Arnold.
2851 Pte. Armstrong.
4803 Pte. Atkins.
4839 Pte. Ashbrook.
4750 Pte. Acheson.
3750 Pte. Bishop.
4712 Pte. Bentcliffe.
5269 Pte. Bates.
4833 Pte. Broadhurst.
2310 15th Hrs., Pte. Browne.
4643 Pte. Brown.
4791 Pte. Brown.
3057 15th Hrs., Pte. Butcher.
2675 11th Hrs., Pte. Brady.
2721 11th Hrs., Pte. Bryant.
4838 Pte. Boothby.
4876 Pte. Barber.
2854 15th Hrs., Pte. Bloom.
4295 Pte. Blackburn.
2466 15th Hrs., Pte. Burbridge.
2292 15th Hrs., Pte. Beer.
4718 Pte. Bradshaw.
4496 Pte. Bodell.
3405 15th Hrs., Pte. Bush.
4069 Pte. Byrne.
4696 Pte. Cowan.
2469 15th Hrs., Pte. Cross.
2653 11th Hrs., Pte Chubb.
2766 11th Hrs., Pte. Corbett.
2619 11th Hrs., Pte. Crisp.
2642 15th Hrs., Pte. Conway.
3513 Pte. Conway.
2761 11th Hrs., Pte. Cracknell.
4728 Pte. Campbell.
4529 Pte. Carson.
4834 Pte. Connor.
4864 Pte. Cox.
4813 Pte. Cutler.
4711 Pte. Collins.
2278 15th Hrs., Pte. Collins.
3166 Pte. E. Clark.
2463 Pte. Clark.
4820 Pte. Clayton.
3030 Pte. Cassidy.
337 15th Hrs., Pte. Chambers.

2802 11th Hrs., Pte. Carroll.
4448 Pte. Dyer.
4783 Pte. Doyle.
4880 Pte. Dempsey.
4821 Pte. Dougan.
2932 11th Hrs., Pte. Dolman.
2690 11th Hrs., Pte. Doggett.
4514 Pte. Dare.
2911 Pte. Dick.
4377 Pte. Earl.
4683 Pte. Etheridge.
4757 Pte. Fausett.
4404 Pte. Flemming.
4835 Pte. Fletcher.
4521 Pte. Fraser.
4732 Pte. Fitten.
4862 Pte. Folbigg.
3102 Pte. Gorsuch.
4875 Pte. Gardner.
4766 Pte. Galloway.
2576 11th Hrs., Pte. Gifford.
3093 Pte. Graham.
4358 Pte. Gale.
2723 15th Hrs., Pte. Gordan.
2505 15th Hrs., Pte. Griffiths.
4694 Pte. Grace.
4776 Pte. Greenhow.
4291 Pte. Holmes.
2993 15th Hrs., Pte. Hales.
4687 Pte. Hatton.
3113 15th Hrs., Pte. Henson.
2838 15th Hrs., Pte. Hurt.
2441 11th Hrs., Pte. Hall.
2471 11th Hrs., Pte. Hickman.
4684 Pte. Hammerton.
3148 Pte. Hill.
2976 11th Hrs., Pte. Hoare.
2450 11th Hrs., Pte. Hamer.
4793 Pte. Harris.
4348 Pte. Henshaw.
4792 Pte. Hindle.
4511 Pte. Harding.
2793 11th Hrs., Pte. Hill.
4881 Pte. Igo.
4828 Pte. Irving.
2912 Pte. Jaffray.

SOUTH AFRICAN WAR

MARCH, 1901.

3364 11th Hrs., Pte. Jennings.
4871 Pte Johnson.
4872 Pte Johnson.
4699 Pte. Johnson.
4861 Pte. Jarvis.
3111 15th Hrs., Pte. Johns.
4816 Pte. Jennings.
4743 Pte. Jackson.
3481 Pte. Kirwin.
4709 Pte. Judd.
3372 Pte. Kenny.
2652 11th Hrs., Pte. Kennie.
3219 Pte. Keogh.
4724 Pte. Keenan.
2947 11th Hrs., Pte. Lambert.
3293 Pte. Lilley.
3110 15th Hrs., Pte. Lewis.
4795 Pte. Leary.
4864 Pte. Lilley.
2831 Pte. Lyons.
4754 Pte. Lahiff.
3351 Pte. McDonnel.
3102 15th Hrs., Pte. McKay.
2750 11th Hrs., Pte. McIlwe.
4809 Pte. McCombe.
4267 Pte. Morgan.
4780 Pte. Moseley.
4848 Pte. Murphy.
2992 15th Hrs., Pte. Murray.
4767 Pte. Mulligan.
4798 Pte. Martin.
4701 Pte. Monks.
2849 15th Hrs., Pte. Mayes.
3138 Pte. McCurry.
2996 Pte. McIlvenny.
4840 Pte. Naden.
4316 Pte. Nixon.
4216 Pte. O'Malley.
4760 Pte. Parker.
4700 Pte Pearce.
4859 Pte. Purton.
2773 15th Hrs., Pte. Puttock.
2744 15th Hrs., Pte. Purchase.
2482 11th Hrs., Pte. Prest.
2733 11th Hrs., Pte. Price.
4877 Pte. Phillips.

4829 Pte. Redmond.
4870 Pte. Reardon.
4837 Pte. Rugg.
4457 Pte. Rhodes.
2963 Pte. Robb.
2493 15th Hrs., Pte. Ritchie.
2355 15th Hrs., Pte. Roberts.
2945 15th Hrs., Pte. Rodford.
4722 Pte. Sheeley.
4665 Pte. Shepperd.
4777 Pte. Small.
4611 Pte. Smith.
4799 Pte. Smith.
4854 Pte. Smith (stowaway).
2659 11th Hrs., Pte. Smith.
2636 11th Hrs., Pte. Smith.
4831 Pte. Sprunt.
3874 Pte. Sparks.
4800 Pte. Sutherland.
2439 11th Hrs., Pte. Sharp.
4945 Pte. Sandwell.
4857 Pte. Skillen.
4729 Pte. Slinger.
2894 15th Hrs., Pte. Southcote.
2667 15th Hrs., Pte. Searing.
2897 Pte. Sutcliffe.
3280 Pte. Selman.
2865 15th Hrs., Pte. Tonge.
4846 Pte. Tabnor (stowaway).
4747 Pte. Thompson.
2354 15th Hrs., Pte. Tomas.
3257 Pte. Ward.
2757 15th Hrs., Pte. Ward.
2853 15th Hrs., Pte. Wakelin.
4277 Pte. Waldron.
4455 Pte. Wall.
4825 Pte. Walters.
4801 Pte. Wolfenden.
4855 Pte. Whitehouse.
4771 Pte. Wilson.
2887 15th Hrs., Pte. Wood.
2943 Pte. Wilkes.
2740 15th Hrs., Pte. Warner.
2693 15th Hrs., Pte. Willesford.
4727 Pte. Walker.
4818 Pte. Walker.

MARCH, 1901.

4474 Pte. Walker.	3009 15th Hrs., Pte. Hughes
3067 Pte. Whats.	drowned at sea during
2953 Pte. Wilcox.	voyage, 8-3-'01).

4TH.—Half rations. Horses 8lbs. corn. Rain again.

5TH.—Rain all day. Since our stay at Piet Retief one squadron (dismounted) has been on outpost every night. Half rations. Horses 8lbs. corn.

7TH.—Rain heavier. Otherwise I think, from what I heard, we should have marched to-morrow.

8TH.—Full ration of biscuits—five—for first time to-day since 28th January. Rain ceased about 10 a.m. Horses 8lbs. corn.

10TH.—Full rations of everything. Horses 4lbs. corn.

11TH.—Ditto.

12TH.—Ditto.

13TH.—Three-quarter rations for men. Horses' rations run out.

14TH.—Beautiful morning for the first time in this camp. No forage. Three-quarter rations of biscuits.

Extract from Divisional Orders:—

"Lieutenant-General French received the following "telegram from Lord Kitchener:—

"I very much regret that you have had such bad "weather. Please express to the troops my appreciation "of their services and endurance under the trying circum-"stances.

"I hope the weather will soon permit you to go on and "move again to complete your successful operations."

15TH.—Marched from Piet Retief at 6 a.m. Still without any forage for horses. Crossed the Assegai River (still in flood) over a trestle bridge, built by Captain Ridout, Royal Engineers. This was a remarkably fine structure, and the longest trestle bridge ever built, as far as I know. Bivouacked at Gooderron after about an eight miles march.

16TH.—Half rations. No forage. Horses very weak. Marched to Annyspruit, near the Slangapies Berg.

MARCH, 1901.

17TH.—Half rations. No forage.
18TH.—Ditto. Rain.
19TH.—Ditto. Two squadrons, 8th Hussars, one squadron, 12th Lancers, and two guns, the whole under Lieutenant-Colonel Clowes, 8th Hussars, marched about five miles in a south-west direction towards Colonel Bullock's convoy, and returned, after establishing communication, with corn for horses.
20TH.—Marched two miles back again in a north-east direction, and camped on the opposite side of the Spruit.
21ST.—Reveillé 3.30 a.m. During the day we only travelled about 12 miles, crossing very bad drifts, before bivouacking at Swartzwater.
22ND.—Crossed the Pongola River, which was now spanned by a pontoon bridge at Jagt Drift, and bivouacked about two miles north of Paul Petersburg. It was officially published to-day that the Pretoria Peace Conference which had been held had terminated unsuccessfully.
23RD.—Reveillé 3.30 a.m. Marched a short way and camped close to the town, which General Dartnell had cleared some time previously. Not one inhabitant remains. The town is a newly built one, prettily situated, and well watered.
24TH.—Marched through the town and bivouacked on the south bank of the Pivaan River, on a bad bit of ground. The river is spanned by a splendidly constructed bridge, somewhat similar in construction to the bridge across the Thames at Oxford.
25TH.—As was generally expected, we moved camp to a healthier spot.
28TH.—I spent the last two afternoons fishing in the river, which teems with fish. To-day I caught about 40 with very primitive tackle. The largest of these we cooked and ate for tea, and, although we took plenty of salt with them, they tasted most insipid. We received news to-day of the severe defeat inflicted on General Delarey by General Babington. Convoy arrived.

MARCH, 1901.

29TH.—Full rations of biscuits and groceries. Captain I. W. Burns Lindow and Lieutenant C. J. M. Lomer embarked for home, invalided.

31ST.—Wet all day.

1ST APRIL.—Two squadrons, 8th Hussars, and one squadron, 10th Hussars, and two guns, went out to escort convoy from Vryheid to camp. Passed over the ridge by the nek overlooking the town, and returned to camp on the 2nd. During the day we heard that we were to eventually proceed to Volksrust. From this camp we are within sight of the mountain on which General Buller earned his V.C.

"A" Squadron occupied a kopje a short distance from camp.

3RD.—The remainder of the regiment proceeded to the kopje occupied by "A" Squadron, which commanded the bridge over the river. The rest of the brigade marched out towards Vryheid. About noon they were seen to be returning, and orders were received for the regiment to rejoin it as it passed, which we did, and, crossing the bridge, we returned to Paulpetersberg and bivouacked two miles east of the town. The brigade camped south of the town on the Nek, as reports had been received that a party of Boers would probably attempt to break through en route to the west.

4TH.—Remained in camp.

5TH.—At mid-day orders were received for the regimental convoy to join the brigade convoy at the Nek, and for the regiment to be prepared to march at midnight against a small commando said to be camped at Dordrecht.

6TH.—Heavy rain commenced to fall about 11 p.m. as we all "stood to." We finally moved about 1.30 a.m. The latest information reported the enemy about ten miles away. The regiment was advance regiment of the brigade, which had left the Nek and followed in our wake. About 3 a.m. a thick mist came on, and our guides mis-led us, otherwise our day's work would have been much more successful. However, at dawn we surprised a Boer patrol

APRIL, 1901.

at a farm house, capturing their ponies, saddles, and rifles; the men managed to escape in the mist to the top of the ridge on which their wagons were parked. The mist lifted between 6 and 7 a.m., and we saw the Boers heading their cattle across a high bluff on our left. About this time the remainder of the brigade came up, and the pursuit commenced, eventually ending in the capture of a few prisoners, 800 oxen, a large number of sheep, some riding ponies, and 12 wagons, which were burned, being unable to take them away. The enemy was chased as far as the Pongola River, which they managed to cross. "B" and "C" Squadrons were well in advance, and were mainly responsible for these captures. The difficult country was all against our making a heavier bag. Some idea of the difficult roads, hills, and ridges over which the pursuit took place may be formed when it was necessary to take the horses out of the pom-pom and haul it up the steep ascents by ropes on returning. Bivouacked at Dordrecht.

7TH.—Returned to bivouac at Paulpetersberg, where we received about two months' mails—22 mail bags for our regimental share.

8TH.—Marched towards Vryheid. Bivouacked at Trekdeel.

9TH.—"B" and "C" Squadrons left at 5.30 a.m. to join Colonel Alderson's Column. Remainder of the brigade marched later and bivouacked about two or three miles east of Vryheid at Nooigedacht.

10TH.—A long day's march. Crossed the Blood River. Saw Majuba Hill in the distance. Bivouacked at Doornberg.

11TH.—Crossed the Buffalo River, still partially in flood, to-day. A wagon and its team of mules was swept some distance down the river, which was running very strongly. Some of the mules were saved by a plucky Kaffir cutting their harness and releasing them. This was not an easy thing to do, as the mules were struggling violently.

April, 1901.

Several of the cattle which we were taking along were drowned whilst swimming across. Bivouacked about five miles from Dundee.

12TH.—Passed under Talana Hill, through the town of Dundee, and marched to Glencoe Station. " A " Squadron entrained at once and proceeded by rail to Ingogo, in Natal. Regimental headquarters remained bivouacked near the station. " B " and " C " Squadrons have not yet re-joined.

Major C. E. Duff proceeded by rail to Pretoria to take command of the 1st Scottish Horse.

16TH.—" B " and " C " Squadrons arrived at Dundee with Colonel Alderson's Column. Part of regimental headquarters moved to Dundee and joined " B " and " C " Squadrons.

17TH.—Remainder of headquarters went to Dundee, where the regiment, minus " A " Squadron, now encamped on the north-east of the town near Talana Hill.

18TH.—A Troop, 35 men, 37 horses, under Lieutenant Allen and Sergeant Walsh, left to proceed by road to Newcastle (Natal).

20TH.—Two troops of " C " Squadron left by road for detachment duty. One, under Captain Van der Byl, proceeding to the Upper Tugela, near Ladysmith, and the other, under Second-Lieutenant Ryder, to Besters Siding, which was about 25 miles from its companion troop at Upper Tugela.

21ST.—No. 4326, Private J. Brunton, died of melancholia at Pietermaritzberg.

25TH.—A large comet, visible at reveillé this morning, appeared daily during the next few days.

1ST MAY.—Headquarters, " B " Squadron, and the half of " C " Squadron left by rail, in trucks, for Volksrust. Passed Majuba Hill and up the steep ascent to Laing's Nek by means of the reversing stations, which, owing to the gradient, are necessary, through the tunnel, and remained the night (a very cold one) on Charlestown

SOUTH AFRICAN WAR

MAY, 1901.

Station platform. Charlestown is the border town of Natal.

2ND.—Arrived at Volksrust, about two miles in the Transvaal, from Natal. Major Henderson re-joined the regiment.

3RD.—Camp well and carefully selected and laid out, as we hear we shall be camped at this place some time. Under canvas for the second time in South Africa. The undermentioned draft of the 11th Hussars, from Cairo, posted to the regiment:—

3260	Cpl. T. Playford.		3544	Pte. W. Hayward.
3714	Lce.-Cpl. W. Swindlehurst.		3606	Pte. F. Higgins.
3542	Pte. R. Adamthwaite.		3651	Pte. J. Hollingsworth.
3560	Pte. A. Ash.		3604	Pte. G. Hunter.
4460	Pte. H. Asher.		4063	Pte. A. Hutchinson.
3411	Pte. A. Baker.		3616	Pte. J. Kelly.
3968	Pte. L. Ball.		3514	Pte. C. Lane.
3492	Pte. A. Ballingall.		4196	Pte. H. Leighton.
3562	Pte. E. Batchelor.		3705	Pte. H. Leonard.
3529	Pte. H. Bentley.		3343	Pte. J. Lindsay.
3335	Pte. G. Berry.		3646	Cpl. A. Holton.
2877	Pte. J. Bishop.		3439	Lce.-Cpl. J. Unwin.
3235	Pte. H. Blakesley.		3605	Pte. J. Lines.
3370	Pte. J. Bomford.		3566	Pte. E. Little.
3356	Pte. A. Bridgman.		3597	Pte. W. Markland.
3600	Pte. J. Brown.		3675	Pte. J. McGovern.
3504	Pte. T. Cobb.		4188	Pte. M. Molloy.
3632	Pte. H. Cole.		2852	Pte. H. Moran.
3596	Pte. W. Coles.		2461	Pte. R. Morgan.
3510	Pte. A. Coomber.		3653	Pte. J. Murphy.
3355	Pte. F. Cox.		3525	Pte. J. North.
3639	Pte. H. Dance.		3546	Pte. J. Oakley.
3482	Pte. F. Davis.		4190	Pte. J. Phelan.
3483	Pte. P. Delaney.		3452	Pte. W. Potter.
3552	Pte. G. Edwards.		3586	Pte. H. Raggett.
3457	Pte. E. Eves.		3395	Pte. W. Robinson.
3462	Pte. F. Farley.		3489	Pte. A. Sadler.
3350	Pte. R. Goldie.		3608	Pte. H. Salter.
3500	Pte. R. Green.		3533	Pte. W. Sherman.
3322	Pte. A. Giustie.		3488	Pte. J. Silverthorn.
3405	Pte. M. Haden.		3367	Pte. W. Smith.
3601	Pte. G. Harris.		3572	Pte. A. Tarrant.
3573	Pte. G. Hawkins.		3648	Lce.-Sgt. J. McGuire.

MAY, 1901.

3494	Cpl. E. Lawrence.	3577	Pte. H. Warwick.
3339	Lce.-Cpl. T. Phillips.	3374	Pte. W. Watson.
3398	Pte. T. Taylor.	3493	Pte. F. Watts.
3432	Pte. J. Telford.	3613	Pte. R. West.
3619	Pte. G. Turner.	3378	Pte. A. White.
3415	Pte. E. Wale.	3418	Pte. C. Wright.
4491	Pte. J. Walsh.	3598	Pte. W. Wright.

Extract from London Gazette, 19th April, 1901 :—

" The undermentioned award is included in the list of " honours up to the 29th December, 1900 :—

" To be Companion of the Most Honourable Order of the Bath:

" Lieutenant-Colonel P. L. Clowes, 8th Hussars."

10TH.—Lieutenant Sir R. W. Levinge embarked for home, invalided.

11TH.—Our camp is on a bare patch of ground, and we have frequent sand storms which penetrate everywhere. The weather, night and morning, is very cold. Ice was found on the water this morning.

14TH.—General Hildyard, Commanding Volksrust Sub-District, inspected the regiment in camp this morning.

Lieutenant P. Stock, Royal Army Medical Corps, who had been on duty with the regiment, joined Charlestown Field Hospital for duty.

16TH.—Two squadrons, " B " and a squadron made up from " A " and " C," four guns, and several companies of the York and Lancaster Regiment, left camp for a short reconnaissance in the Orange Free State (the borders of which are but about two miles away), under command of Colonel Kirkpatrick.

No. 4862, Private G. Folbigg, died at Charlestown of enteric fever.

17TH.—Marched to Ganskraal and came in touch with Colonel Bethune's and Colonel Colville's Columns, which are operating in the north-east of the Free State. During to-day's march we passed through portions of Natal, Transvaal, and Orange Free State Colonies.

MAY, 1901.
18TH.—Took over a large number of cattle and several wagon loads of families of Boers who were still out fighting, from Colonel Colville's Column. Burned veldt all round. The veldt is burned and farms destroyed to prevent (as far as possible) the Boers having any base of supplies in this district.

19TH.—Collected more families to-day, and bivouacked at Quagga Nek.

20TH.—Returned to Volksrust. C.V.S. Wadsworth embarked at Durban for home.

22ND.—" C " and " A " Squadrons and one troop of " B " out on reconnaissance.

27TH.—Half of " B " Squadron and half of " C " Squadron entrained for Glencoe Station en route for Dundee, there to be stationed.

27TH TO 3RD JUNE.—Nothing of moment occurred. Parades daily to drill a number of remounts which joined. Very cold weather is now being experienced.

3RD.—A number of non-commissioned officers and men of the 11th Hussars proceeded to Krugersdorp to join the South African Constabulary:—

11TH.—C.V.S. Wilson attached to the regiment for duty.

12TH.—Half a squadron turned out, under Captain Jennings, and, proceeding to the Klip River Valley, surrounded some farms, in which it had been reported a number of Boers slept every evening.

13TH.—Remainder of the regiment turned out, but no Boers were seen by either party.

No. 4737, Private F. Walker, died of enteric fever at Charlestown.

16TH.—Draft from England arrived.

Draft embarked on s.s. " Manchester Merchant " at Southampton on the 18th May, 1901, and disembarked at Durban 14th June, 1901, and consisted of:—

3631. Sergt. F. Keery.	4462 S.S. G. Harrold.
3764 Cpl. W. Trussell.	5017 S.S. J. Johnson.
4054 Lce.-Cpl. F. Bulcock.	4415 S.S. E. Rainbird.

94 DIARY OF THE

JUNE, 1901.

4029 Tptr. Wetherall.
4029 Pte. J. Abbott.
4597 Pte. W. Ashby.
4938 Pte. A. Ambrose.
4934 Pte. J. Ardis.
4988 Pte. R. Baker.
4923 Pte. R. Bell.
4906 Pte. H. Butler.
5036 Pte. W. Brown.
4954 Pte. J. Basnett.
4966 Pte. A. Brett.
4977 Pte. J. Barry.
5015 Pte. J. Boyle.
4873 Pte. J. Bailey.
5039 Pte. E. Barber.
4892 Pte. E. Bevan.
4980 Pte. W. Brown.
4984 Pte. F. Baynes.
4905 Pte. W. Butcher.
5038 Pte. A. Boyd.
5285 Pte. J. Brightman.
3882 Pte. H. Born.
4856 Pte. W. Carnegie.
5020 Pte. T. Chipperfield.
5032 Pte. J. Cox.
4972 Pte. D. Corbett.
5008 Pte. J. Cooper.
4912 Pte. J. Critchley.
5019 Pte. W. Collier.
5023 Pte. A. Crawford.
4869 Pte. T. Canty.
4916 Pte. G. Chapman.
4982 Pte. A. Crockett.
5051 Pte. F. Cook.
5012 Pte. W. Dawes.
4909 Pte. E. Dickeson.
5042 Pte. H. Deekes.
4949 Pte. H. DeRenzie.
4841 Pte. J. Davidson.
4883 Pte. J. Elmore.
5026 Pte. F. Felstead.
4945 Pte. W. Fletcher.
4958 Pte. J. Fagan.
4919 Pte. W. Foster.
4968 Pte. G. Gadd.
4993 Pte. D. Graham.

4913 Pte. D. Gordon.
4900 Pte. J. Goodall.
4918 Pte. L. Graham.
4740 Pte. E. Gossage.
4603 Pte. B. Gibbins.
4259 Pte. A. Garvey.
4629 Pte. A. Hall.
5009 Pte. T. Hayden.
5043 Pte. W. Harrison.
4836 Pte. W. Heyes.
4566 Pte. H. Hoare.
4946 Pte. F. Haynes.
4985 Pte. H. Holland.
4878 Pte. J. Hanna.
4972 Pte. E. Healy.
5061 Pte. B. Huckle.
5045 Pte. F. Johnson.
4896 Pte. J. Kane.
4920 Pte. F. Kent.
4955 Pte. L. Lambert.
4894 Pte. R. Lindsay.
4979 Pte. J. Lawlor.
4998 Pte. J. Low.
4610 Pte. A. Martin.
4888 Pte. T. McCormick.
4903 Pte. J. McAuley.
5003 Pte. J. Major.
4947 Pte. W. May.
4931 Pte. J. McKenna.
4992 Pte. J. McKeown.
4994 Pte. T. Manley.
4967 Pte. T. McCann.
4991 Pte. F. McCarthy.
4472 Pte. J. Moran.
5043 Pte. G. Nicholson.
4942 Pte. A. Newling.
5025 Pte. A. Pears.
4810 Pte. V. Patrick.
5041 Pte. G. Pitchford.
4981 Pte. W. Proctor.
5011 Pte. J. Quinn.
4824 Pte. G. Rainey.
4776 Pte. T. Ruddy.
4761 Pte. A. Reid.
4974 Pte. E. Robinson.
5004 Pte. G. Rowe.

SOUTH AFRICAN WAR

JUNE, 1901.

4935 Pte. R. Russell.	5001 Pte. J. Uckermann.
5292 Pte. J. Scott.	4782 Pte. R. Waddle.
5016 Pte. W. Smythe.	4850 Pte. J. Walker.
4904 Pte. J. Shrimpton.	4937 Pte. G. Watts.
4381 Pte. G. Taylor.	4990 Pte. R. Wilton.
4959 Pte. E. Tucker.	5293 Pte. T. Wolfendale.
5029 Pte. J. Thomas.	5028 Pte. G. Wright.
4941 Pte. D. Taylor.	5271 Pte. T. Walker.
5037 Pte. J. Todd.	4921 Pte. G. Weston.
5030 Pte. C. Thomas.	

24TH.—Remainder of " C " Squadron left headquarters and proceeded to Dundee in relief of the half of " B " Squadron.

Seventy-five non-commissioned officers and men of " A " Squadron went to Ingogo for duty there.

25TH.—" B " Squadron and 35 men of " A " Squadron left, under Major Wood, for Castrals Nek, to act under Colonel Plumer's orders.

29TH.—The following casualties occurred with Major Wood's party:—

Private Coomber, 11th Hussars, slightly wounded and taken prisoner.

Private Ballingall, 11th Hussars, taken prisoner.

Private Sutherland taken prisoner.

Private Smith taken prisoner.

4TH JULY.—Major D. E. Wood slightly wounded.

9TH.—Major Wood's party returned to Volksrust.

11TH.—120 remounts were received to-day.

Major Wood, Captain Mussenden, Captain Greathed, Lieutenants Jennings, Mort, and Warner, and C.V.S. Wilson, with 175 non-commissioned officers and men, 204 horses, left by rail to join Colonel Rimington's Column at Platrand.

This detachment, whilst with Colonel Rimington, was most successful, and did much good work, being engaged almost every day, operating in the Orange Free State, and sustaining the following casualties :—

JULY, 1901.

13TH.—No. 3490, Private P. Noon, died of wounds received in action near Vrede.

No. 4651, Lance-Corporal W. Woods, slightly wounded near Vrede.

No. 4265, Private R. Winstanley, slightly wounded near Vrede.

No. 3560, Private A. Ash, 11th Hussars, slightly wounded near Vrede.

No. 3586, Corporal C. Gledhill, taken prisoner near Vrede.

No. 2441, Private A. Hall, 11th Hussars, taken prisoner near Verde.

No. 3027, Private W. Crowe, 3rd Hussars, taken prisoner near Vrede.

No. 3427, Private M. McGovern, taken prisoner near Vrede.

No. 4493, Private J. Googan, taken prisoner near Vrede.

The prisoners were subsequently released.

17TH.—No. 3578, Private B. Murtagh, slightly wounded in action near Heilbron.

No. 3292, Private H. McCann, accidentally injured.

27TH.—No. 2355, Sergeant H. Mellish, severely injured by a fall.

No. 4040, Sergeant F. Dunn, severely injured by a fall.

31ST.—Private Higgins severely injured by a fall.

DIARY OF MAJOR WOOD'S DETACHMENT WITH COLONEL RIMINGTON.

13TH.—Started at 6 a.m. and marched to Brakpan. Information was brought in that a Boer convoy was some few miles away. The brigade moved off at once, and after trotting and galloping about six miles, caught sight of it and went for it. Captured 20 wagons, 6 spring carts, 15 Cape carts, and 5 prisoners. Was well sniped by

SOUTH AFRICAN WAR

JULY, 1901.

Boers on hills all around, and sustained the above casualties.

14TH.—Marched all night, and arrived at Brakpan Farm at 3 a.m.; short halt, and on again to Koefontein, where we bivouacked.

15TH.—Marched to Vrede and bivouacked.

16TH.—Started at 8 a.m. About 100 Boers tried to rush "B" Squadron, which was rear guard, but a good shelling sent them to the right about.

17TH.—Started at 4 a.m. to surprise a Boer laager. Thick fog. Marched for two hours and found ourselves back in camp. Left again later. Saw about 100 Boers and chased them, but could not overtake them. Bivouacked at Goedheid.

18TH.—Started at 10 a.m. Acted as left flank guard. Shelled small parties of Boers. Camped at Naauwpoort.

19TH.—Marched at 8.30 a.m. Again shelled small parties before bivouacking at Frankfort.

20TH.—Started at 8 a.m. as right flank patrol. Small parties of Boers were to be seen all round. On our leaving this morning a party of the Australians remained hidden in the town, and on the Boers returning killed two and wounded two. Bivouacked at Klione Spruit.

21ST.—Started at 9 a.m. Marched to Heilbron and bivouacked.

23RD.—Marched at 7 p.m., and arrived near to Krom Spruit at 3 a.m. Could not move again until 9 a.m. owing to the thick mist.

24TH.—Worked in conjunction with Colonel Wing's Column, making a detour to the south. Result: Colonel Wing's Column got 7 prisoners and 10 wagons, and Colonel Rimington's 14 prisoners, 12 wagons, and about 2,000 head of cattle. Returned to Heilbron and bivouacked.

26TH.—Started at 3.30 p.m. Marched to Holland and bivouacked.

27TH.—Started at 6 a.m.

July, 1901.

"B" Squadron, two squadrons Inniskillings, and two guns, under Colonel Wing, marched along the road to beyond Krom Spruit. Some wagons were seen in the distance, and we galloped seven miles after them. Caught and burned seven. Re-joined the brigade at 5 p.m. at Tweefontein. Bivouacked.

28TH.—Started at 7 a.m., and reached Jagersrust at 10.30 a.m. Bivouacked. Very cold. Snow showers. Marched again at 11.30 p.m., and on 29th arrived at Sterkfontein at daybreak. Breakfasted and left wagons there. Came across Boer convoy at Groenvlei, but our two squadrons went away on the right flank and pursued the Boers. Captured 13 wagons and 200 head of cattle. Colonel Rimington's party went on to near Lindley, and captured six wagons, besides accounting for several of the enemy. We also accounted for some and took three prisoners. Returned to Groenvlei and bivouacked.

30TH.—Did not move. A few Boers sniped the camp at night, but did no damage.

31ST.—Started at 2.30 a.m.; marched in a northerly direction. Came across 200 Boers at daybreak. Shelling and sniping all day. Bivouacked at Palmietfontein.

1ST AUGUST.—Started at 7 a.m. and bivouacked at Witpoort.

2ND.—Started at 8.30 a.m. and marched as advanced guard to Heilbron, where bivouacked.

3RD.—Started at 4 a.m. with our two squadrons, Inniskillings, Canadians, and two guns, under Colonel Wood, to look for an imaginary convoy. Only saw ten Boers, and returned to camp.

5TH.—Marched at 5 p.m. in a southerly direction, and arrived on the 6th at Vecht Kop at 1.30 a.m., and bivouacked. Marched again at 11.30 p.m.

7TH.—The column divided into three parts. 8th Hussars detachment went with Colonel Wing on extreme left with two guns and two squadrons of Australians. Arrived at Doornkloof at 8 a.m., and saw a Boer laager not

SOUTH AFRICAN WAR

AUGUST, 1901.

far distant. Galloped for it, and captured 20 wagons, some Cape carts, and 1,500 head of cattle. Boers scooted, accompanied by shells from our gunners. Marched to Blyd Shapp, where we re-joined Colonel Rimington, after covering 50 miles.

8TH.—Started at 9 a.m., and marched as right flank guard to Welgeluk. Saw no Boers, but some of the Inniskillings who remained in a kraal behind the rear guard captured two. Bivouacked.

10TH.—Started at 8 a.m. and marched to Kroonstad. Entrained there for Natal. The driver of the first train struck at Viljohns Drift, and it needed a loaded revolver to persuade him to take the train on.

11TH.—Arrived at Volksrust at 6 p.m.

12TH.—Arrived at Newcastle at 6 a.m. and joined Colonel Pulteney's Column.

This party remained at Newcastle until the 8th of September. There was little to do in that part of the country, and beyond taking part in operations on the 23rd and 29th August, nothing occurred.

7TH.—No. 4333, Private G. Fullerton accidentally injured near Kroonstad.

Extract from Column Orders by Colonel Rimington, Welgeluk, O.R.C., 9th August, 1901 :—

" The Brigadier desires to express to Major Wood, the
" officers, non-commissioned officers, and men of the wing
" of the 8th Hussars his extreme appreciation of the
" excellent work they had done while with his column.
" Their soldierly conduct and good horse management has
" been most exemplary. Their dash has given him the
" keenest pleasure. He wishes them all good luck
" wherever they go.

" B.O. (signed) G. K. ANSELL,
" Staff Officer."

AUGUST, 1901.

REGIMENTAL DIARY—*(Continued).*

13TH.—Captain Lambert, Lieutenant Allen, and 67 men left for Wakkerstroom. The party left Wakkerstroom on the night of the 14th with 50 Mounted Infantry, and marched towards Castrals Nek, surrounding the farms and bringing in families and stock. Returned to Volksrust on the 16th.

20TH.—No. 3143, Private Armstrong, slightly wounded at Pivaanspoort.

23RD.—The part of the regiment at Volksrust left camp at 11 a.m. with a company of infantry and two guns, and marched over Hout Nek to Koch's Farm, which had been fired upon by Boers during the night. We found the owner, Mr. Koch, had been killed, and his son wounded. A Kaffir employed on the farm had been also killed. The remaining members of the family were brought in with the stock of the farm.

25TH.—One hundred and forty-two non-commissioned officers and men, two guns, and one company of the York and Lancaster Regiment marched up Almans Nek Valley. The cavalry, under Captain Lambert, passed through the Nek and returned with 150 ponies and 80 oxen.

28TH.—The regiment, one company York and Lancs, and two guns, marched over Hout Nek to Joubert's Faim, Elandsfontein, bringing in a family and a little stock, returning by De Jager's Nek, after making a reconnaissance extending about 10 miles. During this reconnaissance five men who had been taken prisoners by the Boers at Koch's Farm on the 23rd came in to us. The Boers had taken them to Piet Retief, where they were tried and flogged, and then released. A wire was received in camp to-day from Casualty, Capetown, reporting that No. 3739 Pte. S. Scott, reported missing on the 1st of February, was shot and buried by the Boers at Dernta Pretorius Farm, near Bethel, about the same date as reported missing.

SOUTH AFRICAN WAR

AUGUST, 1901.

30TH.—Draft composed as under embarked on s.s. "Custodian" at Queenstown 27th June, 1901, and disembarked at Durban 26th July, 1901; joined regiment.

Lieut. J. C. Holford.	4865 Pte. R. Kavanagh.
5067 Pte. C. Aldridge.	5031 Pte. T. King.
5085 Pte. J. Brassey.	5060 Pte. J. McDowell.
5049 Pte. J. Bryne.	5044 Pte. W. Mann.
4950 Pte. H. Blundy.	5054 Pte. J. Mallon.
3814 Pte. J. Beadon.	4060 Pte. W. Morgan.
5076 Pte. H. Brown.	5035 Pte. C. Mathers.
5024 Pte. A. Clements.	4805 Pte. M. Moloney.
4960 Pte. E. Colthurst.	4373 Pte. P. Maher.
4997 Pte. A. Cook.	5080 Pte. W. McGregor.
4243 Pte. W. Cullen.	4968 Pte. W. Noble.
5076 Pte. W. Davies.	5048 Pte. G. Philpot.
4961 Pte. C. Fish.	5073 Pte. F. Puttock.
4252 Pte. D. Grimwood.	5065 Pte. W. Seager.
5288 Pte. R. Holland.	5305 Pte. H. Weldon.

31ST.—General Hildyard inspected the camp.

1ST AUGUST.—Extract from "London Gazette" received to-day dated 21st June, 1901:—

"The undermentioned officer is granted the local rank "of Lieutenant-Colonel in South Africa whilst Com- "manding a column.

"Major C. E. Duff, 8th Hussars."

Lieutenant H. M. FitzHerbert and one troop escorted General Hildyard to Moolman's Hoogte.

Ten men acted as escort to Wakkerstroom.

2ND.—Lieutenant Allen and 20 men to Wakkerstroom Nek to meet and escort General Hildyard back to Volksrust.

3RD.—Captain Lambert, with 60 men, left camp at 11 a.m. and visited Kaffir kraals and a farm on the Langberg, returning to camp at 10 a.m. on the 4th, when 40 men left camp at 3 a.m., as support to the party, and to drive in a quantity of stock.

5TH.—Lieutenant FitzHerbert and 40 men proceeded to Newcastle to relieve a troop of the 14th Hussars.

AUGUST, 1901.

7TH.—Second-Lieutenant A. Curell joined the regiment from England.

Captain Lambert and 60 men left camp at dawn and proceeded to some kraals on the Manning Farm, where Boers were reported. No signs of Boers were seen, and the party returned about 9.30 a.m.

8TH.—Captain Lambert and 40 men left camp at 3 a.m., passing over Inketini Nek to Elandshoek to burn kraals belonging to hostile natives, and returned to camp at mid-day.

Lieutenant Holford and 60 men left camp at 7.30 a.m. and escorted a convoy to Wakkerstroom Nek, returning to camp at 4.30 p.m.

9TH.—Small escort to Mount Prospect.

10TH.—Lieutenant Holford and 40 men acted as escort to wagons to Wakkerstroom Nek.

Lieutenant FitzHerbert and 40 men escort to Newcastle.

11TH.—Second-Lieutenant H. F. Partridge joined the regiment from England.

Two small escorts out, one to Mount Prospect, one to Ingogo.

Major D. E. Wood's party passed through Volksrust by rail, en route to Newcastle.

13TH.—Three patrols out, one to Wakkerstroom Nek, and two along the railway towards Zandspruit.

17TH.—Lieutenant Allen, Second-Lieutenant Partridge, and 54 men proceeded to Wakkerstroom.

18TH.—Two small escorts, one to Mount Prospect, one towards Zandspruit.

19TH.—Lieutenant Holford conducted a small reconnaissance.

20TH.—Lieutenant Allen's party returned.

23RD.—Reconnaissance under Lieutenant Holford.

Lieutenant Allen and a troop searched the hills on the right of Wakkerstroom Nek. A party of Boers had been

SOUTH AFRICAN WAR

AUGUST, 1901.

reported, as visiting some kraals close to. He succeeded in capturing three of them and returning to camp.

24TH.—The portion of the regiment at Volksrust left camp under Captain Lambert and proceeded via De Jager's Drift to Elandsfontein, where Boers were reported. There was a little shooting at long ranges, but the enemy got clear away.

27TH.—Two small escorts, one to Joubert's Farm in the Scheilhoek Valley.

29TH.—Lieutenant Holford and eight men left camp at 8.30 p.m., and concealed themselves and horses in a farm called Schoengezicht. It had been reported that a party of Boers came and camped at this farm every night. Soon after midnight a party approached and our men opened fire.

30TH.—The regiment, under Colonel Clowes, turned out at 6 a.m. and proceeded in the direction taken by Lieutenant Holford's party. Found three ponies killed (with blankets and saddles complete) and one rifle. Returned to camp about 1.45 p.m., after scouring the country for five miles.

Extract from Natal District Orders, Newcastle, 30th August, 1901:—

" The following N.C.O. has been brought to the notice
" of the General Commanding-in-Chief, for gallantry in
" the field:—

No. 2933, S.S.M. J. Burns, 8th Hussars.

" When in action at Nondweni, Zululand, on 28th July,
" seized a ridge, the key to the position, and showed great
" gallantry in holding it."

(Army Orders, South Africa, dated 26th August, 1901, para. 1.).

31ST.—About midnight last night, Captain Lambert was ordered out with a strong patrol of 100 N.C.O.'s and men. Information had been received that the Boers were looting the cattle and stock at Joubert's Farm, about five miles

AUGUST, 1901.

distant. This party returned to camp about 9.30 this morning, having found everything safe.

Every evening during the month of August two standing patrols, each consisting of one N.C.O. and three men, patrolled the railway towards Zandspruit all night.

These patrols were strengthened during foggy weather.

Small patrols were engaged almost daily in escorting convoys to Wakkerstroom Nek, or cattle from Volksrust brought in by various columns, to Mount Prospect, en route for Newcastle.

Captain and Adjutant R. Lambert superintended musketry practice for the recruits of the last draft on several occasions during the month. During the past month it is worthy of note, to show what little rest the troops had, that, exclusive of the standing patrols, no fewer than 16 patrols under officers and 14 under N.C.O.'s were called upon for duty during the month.

1ST SEPTEMBER.—" A " Squadron stood to arms, horses ready saddled, from 6.30 p.m. yesterday until nearly midnight, but were not called upon to turn out. The same squadron escorted a convoy to Wakkerstroom Nek to-day.

All available mounted men left in camp turned out under Captain Lambert at noon to reconnoitre the Scheilhoek Valley, returning at 7 p.m.

3RD.—Lieutenant Holford and two troops escorted a convoy to Wakkerstroom Nek.

4TH.—Three troops of " A " Squadron, under Lieutenant Holford, escorted a convoy from Wakkerstroom Nek to Volksrust.

Lieutenant FitzHerbert and one troop of " B " Squadron turned out at 11.30 p.m. and reconnoitred the ground towards Opperman's Kraal.

6TH.—Sergeant Wilkes and six men proceeded to the Scheilhoek Valley to protect farm hands while engaged in cutting mealies.

Lieutenants Allen and FitzHerbert and 75 men proceeded to Wakkerstroom.

SOUTH AFRICAN WAR

SEPTEMBER, 1901.

Three standing night patrols were required to-night, Boers having been reported at Mount Dorset.

7TH.—Extra precautions were taken against night attacks. Brigadier-General Bullock visited the camp and inspected the method adopted in manning the trenches and sangars.

Three standing night patrols.

8TH.—Captain Jennings, Lieutenant Holford, and 89 men marched to Wakkerstroom.

Major Wood, with the three officers and 133 rank and file, rejoined Head Quarters from Newcastle.

About 9 a.m. the troops were ordered to stand ready to turn out at a moment's notice. This, however, ended by Captain Jennings taking a party to Wakkerstroom.

11TH.—Captain Mussenden, Lieutenant Partridge, and 68 rank and file, marched to Wakkerstroom.

Captain Jennings, Lieutenant Holford, and 70 rank and file rejoined Head Quarters from Wakkerstroom (see 8th September, 1901).

12TH.—Sergeant Pitchforth and 12 men escorted a post cart to Wakkerstroom Nek.

13TH.—Two troops of " A " Squadron, under Captain Jennings, left camp at 8 a.m. to reconnoitre the Buffalo Valley.

Two troops of " A " Squadron, under Lieutenant Holford, escort to convoy to Nek.

14TH.—Two troops of " A " Squadron, under Lieutenant Holford, escorted convoy to Nek.

18TH.—Captain Jennings, Lieutenant Warner, and 65 men and 69 horses proceeded to Wakkerstroom.

Very cold and misty weather has been experienced since the 14th inst.

The three standing night patrols remained out until the mist lifted in the mornings, generally about 9.30 a.m.

19TH.—Weather so bad that standing patrols were out day and night.

SEPTEMBER, 1901.

20TH.—An escort of all available N.C.O.'s and men in camp escorted a convoy to the Nek.

Captain Jennings and party returned from Wakkerstroom.

21ST.—Owing to the continued bad weather very strong escorts were required to accompany convoys. The escort to-day under Lieutenant Holford was 100 rank and file strong.

23RD.—One officer, 60 rank and file, escort to convoy.

24TH.—An escort of the same strength as yesterday out to-day.

25TH.—Lieutenant Holford and 80 men escort to convoy.

Corporal Bowes and 12 men turned out at 11.30 a.m. to intercept five Boers who were endeavouring to drive ponies in from Scheilhoek Valley to their outposts at Alleman's Nek. A few shots were exchanged, and the Boers retired without succeeding in capturing any.

27TH.—Lieutenant Warner and 60 men on escort duty.

Lieutenant Holford and 30 men patrolled the Scheilhoek Valley.

28TH.—Sergeant Keery and 12 men escorted medical officers during their inspection of the sources of water supplies to the Volksrust and Charlestown districts.

29TH.—The undermentioned non-commissioned officers and men of a draft arrived at Cape Town and disembarked for Durban and joined Regimental Head Quarters 29th September, 1901, being posted to Squadrons as follows :—

"A" Squadron.

5086	Lce.-Cpl. J. Webster.		5112	Pte. G. Holmes.
5115	Pte. J. Brandford.		4359	Pte. H. Iliffe.
3484	Pte. P. Coleman.		4380	Pte. H. Lilley.
5122	Pte. H. Cox.		5103	Pte. A. Lee.
5095	Pte. E. Glasgow.		5105	Pte. H. Robinson.
5098	Pte. C. Grainger.		5114	Pte. T. Smith.
5091	Pte. A. Hall.		5077	Pte. H. Woodward.

SEPTEMBER, 1901.
"B" Squadron.

5090	Lce.-Cpl. H. Highley.	5121	Pte. E. Hawes.
5064	S.S. H. Jones.	5125	Pte. W. Ives.
5120	Pte. W. Beasley.	5111	Pte. J. Mason.
5050	Pte. R. Barry.	5068	Pte. A. Mastin.
5057	Pte. G. Day.	2974	Pte. J. Moss.
4915	Pte. G. Downs.	5127	Pte. A. Smith.
5100	Pte. J. Hayes.	5088	Pte. H. Strover.

30TH.—Sergeant Harvey and 12 men, Lieutenant Holford and 20 men acted as escorts for purposes similar to those on the 28th inst.

Lieutenant-Colonel C. E. Duff, with 1st Scottish Horse, slightly wounded at Moedwil.

During the month of September, 18 officers and 4 N.C.O.'s escorts or patrols were engaged, chiefly in acting as escorts to convoys proceeding to Wakkerstroom.

The very misty nights and early mornings necessitated the sending out of three standing patrols on nineteen occasions during the month.

2ND OCTOBER.—All available N.C.O.'s and men in camp were required to-day to act as escort to convoy proceeding to Wakkerstroom.

3RD.—Captain Jennings, with 50 men, proceeded to Botha's Pass, acting as escort to R.E. during the erection of blockhouses.

4TH.—Lieutenant Holford and 60 men escort to convoy.

Sergeant Rayfield and 12 men turned out at midnight and proceeded to some Kaffir kraals about four miles distant, where Boers were supposed to sleep each night.

5TH.—Sergeant's patrol returned about 9 a.m. and reported having seen a few Boers leaving kraals at least four miles away, soon after sunrise.

8TH.—A patrol under Lieutenant Holford left camp to escort a convoy to the Nek; owing to the severity of the weather the convoy was unable to proceed, and the escort returned to camp.

9TH.—Second-Lieutenant Warner and 30 men escort to convoy.

OCTOBER, 1901.

10TH.—Lieutenant Holford, 31 men and 35 horses, left Volksrust to be temporarily stationed at Castral's Nek.

Captain Jennings and 40 men escort to convoy.

No. 5041, Pte. G. Pitchford died of disease at Mooi River.

12TH.—Captain Jennings and a party of N.C.O.'s and men left camp at midnight, returning

13TH—at 2.30 p.m., leaving again the same evening at 7 p.m. and being relieved by Captain Lambert, with a machine gun and an equal number of men at

14TH—9.30 a.m., who was relieved, in turn,

15TH—at 3 p.m. by Captain Jennings.

16TH.—Similar reliefs.

17TH.—Captain Jennings' party at Wakkerstroom Nek was attacked about daybreak by a small party of Boers, who were driven back. No. 4127, Pte. M. Frain was severely wounded in the wrist.

18TH.—Sergeant Harvey and 12 men on escort duty.

19TH.—One N.C.O. and 12 men, escort duty.

Two privates escort—no corporals available.

20TH.—Lieutenant-Colonel P. L. Clowes left Volksrust for England.

One sergeant and 12 men escorted a small convoy to the Nek.

22ND.—Captain Jennings returned to camp, bringing in the detached outposts from Wakkerstroom, Crawford's, and Moll's Nek. Since the 12th inst. these neks have been held by troops of the regiment to prevent the enemy, who are being driven to the west by mobile columns, from breaking through and passing into the Free State.

24TH.—Second-Lieutenant Warner and 40 men escorted gun to Nek.

25TH.—Lieutenant Mort and 50 men escort duty.

27TH.—Captain Jennings and 50 men escort duty.

28TH.—One N.C.O. and 15 men escorted two ambulances from the Nek.

30TH.—One N.C.O. and 15 men escort duty.

SOUTH AFRICAN WAR

OCTOBER, 1901.

31ST.—One N.C.O. and 15 men escort duty.

No. 4,209, Pte. T. Dawson drowned in the Buffalo River.

On fifteen days during the month three standing night patrols were required, and there were only six days on which no escorts were furnished.

1ST NOVEMBER.—Second-Lieutenant Warner and 50 men escort duty.

2ND.—Eighty horses in good condition were handed to the 18th and 19th Hussars, who returned eighty horses incapable of trekking.

Second-Lieutenant Curell took thirty of the latter to Mount Prospect, en route for Newcastle, returning with 30 fit horses.

5TH.—Second-Lieutenant Warner and 40 men escort duty.

6TH.—One N.C.O. and ten men escorted some cattle from Zandspruit to Volksrust.

7TH.—Second-Lieutenant Malet and 40 men escort duty.

8TH.—Lieutenant Mort and 40 men escort duty.

10TH.—Captain Jennings and 60 men escort duty.

13TH.—Second-Lieutenant Warner and 70 men escort duty.

14TH.—One N.C.O. and eight men held the Nek during the time a battery of Artillery was passing through.

15TH.—Second-Lieutenant Warner and 31 men left camp to relieve Lieutenant Holford at Castral's Nek.

Second-Lieutenant Curell and 20 men took over wagons and prisoners from an escort which arrived at Wakkerstroom Nek, and conducted them to Volksrust Head Quarters.

17TH.—Owing to a rumour that the enemy, whose outposts were seen daily at Alleman's Nek, would attempt to cross the line between Vanderchief Bridge and Duckpond Blockhouse, a party of dismounted men, under Lieutenants Mort and Curell, was sent out at 6 p.m. to fill up a

NOVEMBER, 1901.

breach in the defences of the line between these posts. This party returned shortly after daybreak next day, no attempt having been made.

18TH.—Lieutenant Holford rejoined from Castral's Nek.

Sergeant Keery and 8 men patrolled the line between the posts mentioned on the 17th, from 7 p.m. till shortly after midnight.

20TH.—A sergeant and 12 men escort to General Lyttelton.

21ST.—Two officers, 91 N.C.O.'s and men, joined Head Quarters from Ingogo, having been relieved by the 14th Hussars.

22ND.—Lieutenant Mort and 40 men escort duty.

23RD.—Second-Lieutenant Howard and 60 men left camp to occupy two posts—Mabola and Amsterdam—on the Wakkerstroom—Piet Retief blockhouse line.

Lieutenant Holford and 40 men escort duty.

25TH.—Sergeant Pitchforth and 10 men escorted wagons towards Zandspruit.

Second-Lieutenant Curell and 30 men escort duty.

26TH.—About midnight every available N.C.O. and man left camp and proceeded rapidly to Charlestown, which was said to be attacked. Party returned to camp about 5 a.m. next day, having seen no sign of the enemy.

27TH.—Lieutenant Mort and 30 men escort to convoy.

Fifteen men and 25 horses left to join " B " Squadron (Colonel Pulteney's Column).

Three standing night patrols were furnished 29 times during the month.

1ST DECEMBER.—" B " Squadron details (Lieutenant Curell) joined Head Quarters from Newcastle.

2ND.—Lieutenant Mort and 30 men left camp to act as escort to Brigadier-General Bullock during his tour of inspection of the Wakkerstroom—Piet Retief blockhouse line.

3RD.—One N.C.O. and 12 men escort duty.

DECEMBER, 1901.
Day patrol out owing to the misty weather.
4TH.—A sergeant and 12 men escort duty.
5TH.—A sergeant and 12 men escort duty.
6TH.—Lieutenant Holford and 20 men left camp at 7 a.m. to patrol the line towards Zandspruit.
A sergeant and 12 men escort duty.
7TH.—Lieutenant Holford's party returned to camp at 7 a.m.
A sergeant and 15 men escort duty to 60 wagons to the Nek.
8TH.—Lieutenant Holford and 30 men escort duty.
9TH.—Lieutenant Holford and 38 men left camp to patrol the Scheilhoek Valley.
11TH.—Captain Viscount Garnock and 50 men escort duty.
13TH.—Captain Viscount Garnock, Second-Lieutenant Malet and 50 men acted as escort to the York and Lan. Regiment, taking with them five days' supplies.
One N.C.O. and 13 men escort duty.
17TH.—No. 5111, Pte. J. Mason died at Charlestown Hospital of enteric fever.
Lieutenant Mort and 45 men escort duty.
18TH.—One corps and five men escorted a party of R.E. detailed to repair the telegraph line.
Sergeant Pitchforth and 10 men on night patrol on Manning Farm.
19TH.—Lieutenant Mort and 60 men proceeded to Newcastle for remounts.
A sergeant and seven men escort duty.
23RD.—Lieutenant Holford and 20 men acted as escort along the Iketini—Quagga blockhouse line.
Captain Lambert and 50 men left camp suddenly at noon, 25 Boers having been reported some distance away. This party returned about 8 p.m., having seen no signs of the enemy, and having covered over 50 miles of country.
The following draft joined headquarters at Volksrust

DECEMBER, 1901.

on the 23rd December, 1901, having embarked at Queenstown on the 28th November, 1901, and disembarked at Durban on the 21st December, 1901:—

"A" Squadron.

6175	Sergt. Marchant.		5194	Pte. G. Kingaby.
5267	Pte. J. Allison.		5237	Pte. A. Loftus.
4135	Pte. E. Burns.		4619	Pte. R. Mack.
5133	Pte. G. Coles.		5096	Pte. W. Mansfield.
5131	Pte. E. Cooper.		5223	Pte. E. Morris.
5268	Pte. A. Crowhurst.		5255	Pte. W. Perry.
5259	Pte. E. Ely.		5130	Pte. G. Pountney.
5156	Pte. G. Greenwood.		5072	Pte. W. Simmonds.
5053	Pte. M. Jordan.		5336	Pte. J. Theobald.
4302	Pte. G. Jurdison.		3644	Tptr. A. Hughes.

"B" Squadron

5188	Pte. C. Allard.		4715	Pte. R. Mills.
5165	Pte. C. Bullen.		5234	**Pte. D. O'Donnell.**
3548	Pte. J. Cross.		4898	Pte. T. Ruddle.
3548	Pte. J. Coss.		5225	Pte. H. Searing.
5249	Pte. T. Exall.		5039	Pte. G. Slow.
5221	Pte. H. King.		5196	Pte. W. Sumpster.
4726	Pte. F. Maud.		5189	Pte. W. Taylor.
5129	Pte. G. Mayman.		2915	Pte. C. Waller.
5253	Pte. A. Mitchell.		5178	Pte. A. Walker.

"C" Squadron.

3697	Sergt. H. Hiorns.		5035	Pte. J. Few.
5204	Pte. J. Barnes.		5178	Pte. T. Goddard.
5168	Pte. C. Donohoe.		5228	Pte. W. Gibbs.
5277	Pte. O. Griffiths.		5173	Pte. S. Symonds.
5185	Pte. W. Irving.		5182	Pte. T. Smart.
5250	Pte. J. Jones.		5051	Pte. W. Reed.
5245	Pte. E. Palmer.		5218	Pte. H. Underwood.
5175	Pte. F. Sill.		4093	S.S. H. Moore.
5059	Pte. C. Bailey.		4512	Saddler W. Hodgkins.
5118	Pte. F. Bird.			

24TH.—One sergeant and nine men escort duty.

Lieutenant-Colonel C. E. Duff rejoined and took over command of the regiment.

25TH.—One sergeant and nine men escorted an ammunition wagon to the Nek.

DECEMBER, 1901.
26TH.—Lieutenant Mort and 25 men escort duty.
To relieve the monotony some sports were organized and came off to-day, and were a great success.
The Green Hill standing night patrol was strengthened to one N.C.O. and seven men, with orders to patrol the railway line during the whole night.
27TH.—Lieutenant Woods and 50 men left to strengthen Captain Viscount Garnock's party (at Botha's Pass), which left on the 13th inst. for five days.
29TH.—Thirty-one men rejoined Head Quarters from the posts on the Wakkerstroom—Piet Retief blockhouse line.
30TH.—Lieutenant Holford's party, which left on the 23rd, rejoined Head Quarters.
31ST.—Last draft of recruits practised in musketry.
Second-Lieutenant J. C. Brutton left to join Captain Garnock's party.
1ST JANUARY, 1902.—Lieutenant Mort and 20 men acted as escort to convoy.
2ND.—Lieutenant Woods, with 20 men, left camp at noon, Boers being reported
3RD—at Johnson's Farm, about 8 miles distant. He was successful in capturing four.
About 7 p.m. another party of 20 men turned out, under Lieutenant Mort,, and another at 2 a.m. These two parties co-operated in thoroughly searching the ground round about the farm, returning to camp about 6 a.m., having seen no further trace of the enemy.
5TH.—One sergeant and 10 men escort duty.
6TH.—The Green Hill patrol, under Corporal Johnson, brought in seven armed surrendered Burghers this morning—part of the Alleman's Nek Boer Force.
Lieutenant Woods and 20 men escort duty.
7TH.—A sergeant and 12 men left to bring in a surrendered burgher and his family and belongings.
8TH.—Second-Lieutenant Hindley and 20 men escort duty.

JANUARY, 1902.

10TH.—Lieutenant Mort and 20 men escort duty.

11TH.—Three escorts out, one consisting of one N.C.O. and 6 men; another of one officer and 20 men; and the third of one N.C.O. and 11 men, as escort, by rail, to Boer prisoners to Durban.

13TH.—Lieutenant Woods and 20 men proceeded to Moll's Nek, where Boers were reported; returned without finding any trace of them.

16TH.—Lieutenant Mort, Lieutenants Woods and Hindley, with 110 N.C.O.'s and men, left to join General Bullock's column in the Free State.

Five officers and 127 rank and file of the 3rd Hussars, from India, attached to the regiment for duty.

17TH.—Twenty-three rank and file 3rd Hussars joined.

18TH.—Twenty-three men proceeded mounted to join the Squadrons "A" and "C" on Botha's Pass—Verde blockhouse line.

22ND.—Columns were operating about this time in the Pongola Bosch, driving the Boers westward. The three neks E. and S.E. of Volksrust, viz., Wakkerstroom, Crawford's, and Moll's Nek, appear to be the only routes by which Boers could break through to the north. These were therefore occupied by five officers and 104 N.C.O.'s and men of the 3rd Hussars, and one officer and 37 men (dismounted) of the 8th Hussars and a number of infantry. No attempt was made to break through, and the majority of the troops returned on the 28th. Heavy rains fell during the greater part of the time these troops were out. The duty in camp was very heavy. With every man doing guards they did not average one night in bed, *i.e.*, off duty, although a troop of 28 N.C.O.'s and men of the 14th Hussars were sent to assist in the defence of the camp.

25TH.—Lieutenant Partridge passed through from Newcastle with remounts for "B" Squadron.

27TH.—One officer and 11 men returned from Moll's Nek.

SOUTH AFRICAN WAR

JANUARY, 1902.

One officer and 23 dismounted men returned from one of the other neks.

28TH.—Three officers and 43 men returned from the neks. The whole of the remainder of the troops still out are to remain until a line of blockhouses is erected.

2ND FEBRUARY.—The detachment of the 3rd Hussars left the regiment.

One sergeant, 22 men, and 33 horses left for Laing's Nek, to be stationed there for duty.

3RD.—No. 4903, Pte. J. McAuley died at Charlestown of enteric fever.

One sergeant and twenty men escort duty.

4TH.—Lieutenant Holford, one sergeant, and 29 men, with 43 horses, left for Laing's Nek.

One sergeant and 6 men escort duty.

No. 5118, Pte. F. Bird died at Heilbron of enteric fever.

Sergeant Keery and 28 men of " A " Squadron rejoined Head Quarters.

5TH.—One Sergeant and 6 men escort duty.

No. 4908, Pte. G. Gadd, died at Charlestown Hospital of enteric fever.

6TH.—One sergeant and 6 men escort duty.

7TH.—One sergeant and 6 men escort duty.

10TH.—The following non-commissioned officers and men of the 11th Hussars sailed from Alexandria, Egypt, landed at Durban on the 3rd February, 1902, and joined the regiment at Volksrust on the 10th February, 1902, and were posted to squadrons as stated:—

"A" Squadron.

3265 Sgt. M. F. Fryer.	4398 Pte. W. C. Bull.
4235 Cpl. W. Vearncombe.	4542 Pte. J. Carlon.
3830 Pte. C. Abbott.	4356 Pte. F. Cockley.
3261 Pte. J. Ashbury.	4498 Pte. M. Conyers.
3745 Pte. H. Bailey.	4445 Pte. M. Cowan.
3860 Pte. W. Bell.	4408 Pte. E. Daniels.
4586 Pte. G. Brannagan.	4361 Pte. T. Dixon.
3799 Pte. H. Brown.	3553 Pte. C. Duggan.

DIARY OF THE

FEBRUARY, 1902.

4353	Pte.	R. Fagan.
4488	Pte.	J. Fisher.
3817	Pte.	C. H. Freegard.
4394	Pte.	T. H. Freeman.
4194	Pte.	W. J. Gavin.
4502	Pte.	J. Gordon.
4501	Pte.	A. Hamilton.
4400	Pte.	W. Hayhurst.
3574	Pte.	A. M. Hornsby.
3705	Pte.	A. Ives.
4446	Pte.	A. Kirkwood.
4359	Pte.	E. McCabe.
4549	Pte.	D. J. McDonald.
3722	Pte.	W. J. McPherson.
4354	Pte.	D. Miller.
4531	Pte.	T. Moss.
4192	Pte.	A. J. Newton.
3843	Pte.	E. A. Palmer.
3770	Pte.	A. G. Randall.
4443	Pte.	J. Rivers.
4570	Pte.	J. Rutherglen.
4349	Pte.	J. R. Sedgwick.
4369	Pte.	R. J. Skyrme.
3909	Pte.	W. Smith.
4439	Pte.	D. A. Swanson.
3581	Pte.	C. H. Renton.
4460	Pte.	P. H. Vinten.
3821	Pte.	J. Wain.
3589	Pte.	G. J. Welsh.
4350	Pte.	G. A. Wilson.
4403	Pte.	W. Pirie.

"B" Squadron.

3134	Sgt.	A. Gilman.
3174	Cpl.	J. Conrad.
2399	Cpl.	H. Grigg.
3571	Pte.	A. A. Stevens.
4560	Pte.	H. J. Boarne.
3657	Pte.	W. Bremner.
3437	Pte.	J. W. Brown.
4500	Pte.	F. Bullimore.
3610	Pte.	A. W. Challis.
3687	Pte.	A. Cowen.
4405	Pte.	J. Cooper.
3850	Pte.	H. J. Cramp.
3746	Pte.	D. A. Davies.
4424	Pte.	D. A. Downing.
4566	Pte.	W. Eagles.
3853	Pte.	R. Ferrier.
4345	Pte.	J. Fletcher.
4521	Pte.	J. A. Fleet.
3503	Pte.	J. Gaynor.
3918	Pte.	A. Goodison.
4435	Pte.	J. Grant.
3478	Pte.	A. J. Hatcher.
3818	Pte.	H. Head.
3862	Pte.	G. S. Hinds.
3539	Pte.	T. Huggins.
4567	Pte.	G. W. Jackson.
4389	Pte.	T. Little.
4481	Pte.	A. J. McCormack.
3789	Pte.	J. McGuire.
4493	Pte.	W. J. Melhuish.
3444		F. Mitchell.
4395	Pte.	F. Munday.
3814	Pte.	D. Nicol.
4485	Pte.	A. Perry.
4553	Pte.	T. A. Ransom.
4546	Pte.	T. A. Roberts.
4363	Pte.	S. F. Saunders.
4162	Pte.	S. Shove.
4476	Pte.	D. Smith.
3558	Pte.	J. H. Stevens.
4565	Pte.	P. B. Tait.
3880	Pte.	F. H. Tucker.
3875	Pte.	H. E. Walker.
3670	Pte.	C. Wickenden.
3960	Pte.	H. Wilson.

"C" Squadron.

3149	Sgt.	C. B. Dyke.
2792	Sgt.	W. Hollerton.
3883	Pte.	C. Abbott.
4366	Pte.	C. Anderson.
4532	Pte.	J. Ashworth.
3927	Pte.	M. Ashworth.

SOUTH AFRICAN WAR

FEBRUARY, 1902.

4414 Pte. H. Bayley.	4404 Pte. W. Johnstone.
4543 Pte. J. Boyd.	4594 Pte. W. McDonald.
3863 Pte. J. Brooks.	4383 Pte. J. McCracken.
3772 Pte. W. Brown.	3854 Pte. F. McLaughlan.
3858 Pte. J. Cameron.	3333 Pte. T. Mellay.
4429 Pte. G. Chatteris.	4360 Pte. J. Mitchell.
4508 Pte. T. Conolly.	3580 Pte. A. Neale.
3672 Pte. H. Corder.	3896 Pte. A. C. D. Oliver.
4486 Pte. J. Dagworthy.	4572 Pte. F. J. Pitt.
3787 Pte. E. Devey.	3664 Pte. J. Reynolds.
4387 Pte. W. Downs.	3443 Pte. F. Roper.
4527 Pte. J. J. Ellis.	4165 Pte. J. Icart.
4562 Pte. J. Finnigan.	4409 Pte. A. Sidders.
4381 Pte. W. Forrest.	3734 Pte. W. Smith.
4377 Pte. G. Gale.	4372 Pte. W. Stoker.
4396 Pte. C. Gill.	4468 Pte. T. K. Tarrant.
3834 Pte. H. Hall.	4510 Pte. W. Watson.
3796 Pte. C. Hawkins.	3584 Pte. W. J. Willicombe.
4447 Pte. A. Hill.	4551 Pte. C. Young.
3840 Pte. J. Impett.	

11TH.—One sergeant and six men escort duty.

12TH.—One sergeant and six men escort duty.

Lieutenant Lomer and 30 men turned out at 10 p.m. to prevent the Boers who are known to be at Alleman's Nek breaking across the line northwards.

13TH.—One sergeant and six men escort duty.

No. 3381, Lance-Corporal F. Battrick, died at Charlestown of enteric fever.

14TH.—One sergeant and six men escort duty.

No. 4,462, S.S. G. Harrold, died at Charlestown of enteric fever.

15TH.—Lieutenant Mort and Lieutenant Lomer, with 50 men, left for Wakkerstroom.

16TH.—Lieutenant Mort and his party returned.

Captain Jennings, Lieutenant Hindley, and 40 men, with 53 horses, rejoined from the Piet Retief blockhouse line.

17TH.—One sergeant and six men escort duty.

No. 5008, Pte. J. Cooper died at Charlestown of enteric fever.

MARCH, 1902.

8TH MARCH.—Detachments of "A" and "B" Squadrons, under Captain Mort and Lieutenants Woods and Hindley, marched from Volksrust to Standerton via Paardekop, and Platrand, arriving at Standerton on the 9th. "B" Squadron was there, having come in with Colonel Pulteney.

No. 3481, Pte. J. Kirwan died at Harrismith of wounds received on the 26th February, 1902.

17TH.—Head Quarters and details of "A" and "B" Squadrons marched from Volksrust to Pardekop en route to join Colonel Wing's Column. Major Lord Garnock was in command of the party.

18TH.—Marched to Platrand.

19TH.—Marched to Standerton. Colonel C. E. Duff rejoined. All the regiment was thus concentrated here, with the exception of the detachment under Major Henderson with Colonel Nixon's column.

20TH.—Marched to Leeuwspruit en route to Morgonzon. Lieutenant Warner arrived at Standerton with troop from Castral's Nek.

21ST.—Marched to Morgonzon, joining Colonel Wing's column, composed of 18th Hussars, 19th Hussars, Australians, West Australian Mounted Infantry, two guns, and a pom-pom.

22ND.—Marched to Bethel with supplies for the Garrison there.

Australians had sharp rear guard action. Remained at Bethel until 25th, when we left at 3.30 a.m. and marched to Verbliding, near Standerton, having taken part with Colonels Park's and Williams' Columns in a drive on to the railway line.

Remained in camp until the 30th, when we marched to Leeuwspruit. Night marched at 11 p.m. Short fight near the blockhouse line. Start of drive on to Ermelo—Carolina blockhouse line.

31ST.—Bivouacked at Mooifontein.

1ST APRIL.—The regiment is now with Colonel Wing's

Column. Marched to-day at 7 a.m., moving in extended order on the right of the column. Squadrons operated about 1½ miles apart, searching every farm. Saw no Boers. Bivouacked at Sukkelaar.

2ND.—Regiment on the left of the column. Saw about 25 Boers near the end of the day. Found two wounded Boers in a farm. Bivouacked at Springbokfontein.

3RD.—Marched at 7 a.m. Regiment on the right. Saw nothing. Bivouacked at Reit Vlei.

4TH.—Marched to Ermelo, of which only the church remains standing. End of the drive. Result of the drive —28 Boers captured.

5TH.—Joined Colonel Park's Column, as Colonel Duff was found to be senior to Colonel Wing. Column consisted of Urmiston's Mounted Infantry, 4th Mounted Infantry, Manchester Regiment, two guns, one pom-pom.

6TH.—Marched to Welgelegen. Regiment and Mounted Infantry extended in front of column saw about 80 Boers, who retired. Found several farms full of food stuffs and forage. One farm, besides containing about five women and as many children, contained enough prepared food for a good meal for about 50 men, evidently ready for the enemy on our passing by. First experience of a perimeter camp.

7TH.—Marched to De Goedevervachting. Colonel Wing's Column, on the right, passed close to Lake Chrissie. No Boers.

8TH.—Marched through Carolina to Roodepoort, where we bivouacked at 11 a.m.

No. 4349, Private J. Sedgwick, died at Standerton of enteric fever.

9TH.—Marched at 6 a.m. along Wonderfontein Blockhouse line to Lillefontein, then on to Nooitgedacht, where we bivouacked at 1 p.m.

10TH.—Marched to Eikeboom. Bivouacked at 2 p.m.

11TH.—Marched to Rhenosterfontein and formed up

APRIL, 1902.

for drive to Standerton—Elandsfontein line. Squadrons were split up into posts, each of ten non-commissioned officers and men 150 yards apart. Each post was entrenched at night by putting wagons every 150 yards, with barbed wire in between.

12TH.—Marched at 6.30 a.m. along the South African Constabulary blockhouse line (Brug Spruit to Vaal Station) to Diepspruit, where we entrenched on arriving at 4 p.m.

13TH.—Started at 6.30 a.m. in a thunderstorm, and marched along the line of blockhouses to Wildebeestfontein. Entrenched at 4 p.m.

14TH.—Started at 6 a.m. and marched along the line of blockhouses to Vaal Station, arriving at 6 p.m. The regiment bivouacked all together. Result of the drive—1 killed, 1 wounded, and 132 prisoners.

15TH.—Same camp.

16TH.—Started at 6 a.m. and marched along the South African Constabulary blockhouse line to Vaal Bank, where we bivouacked.

Colonel C. E. Duff received orders to take over command of Colonel Wing's Column, as Colonel Wing had broken his collar bone.

Major Lord Garnock took over command of the regiment.

17TH.—Marched at 7 a.m. to Witkyk, where we offsaddled for an hour, and then proceeded to Onverwacht, entrenched and bivouacked.

Colonel Park's Column, followed by Colonel Duff's, strengthened the South African Constabulary blockhouse line, which formed the eastern boundary of the drive.

18TH.—Marched at 6.30 a.m. Bivouacked and entrenched at Meyers' Farm, on the Steinkoolspruit.

19TH.—Marched at 6.30 a.m. to Naaupoort. Bivouacked and entrenched.

20TH.—Marched at 6.30 a.m. to Whitbank Station, where a halt was made for a short time. The column

APRIL, 1902.
afterwards moved to Groot Oliphant's Station, bivouacked and entrenched. Result of this drive, 28 prisoners taken.

21ST.—Started at 11.30 a.m. and marched to Whitbank Station, where we off-saddled till the wagons came, when we proceeded to Naaupoort and joined Colonel Duff's Column (8th, 18th and 19th Hussars).

22ND.—Started at 6.30 a.m. and marched to Steinkoolspruit, where we off-saddled for two hours, and then went on as left flank guard to Boschras, marching in a heavy thunderstorm.

23RD.—Started at 6 a.m. and marched to Bethel.

24TH.—Marched to Wildebeestfontein, taking Bethel garrison away. "B" Squadron, who were rear guard, saw about 200 Boers, and "A" Squadron were sent back in support. Boers kept off.

Detachment consisting of Major Henderson, Captains Jennings and Van der Byl, Lieutenants Lomer, Holford, and Ryder, and parts of "A" and "C" Squadrons, rejoined Head Quarters from Colonel Nixon's Column. Major Henderson took over command of the regiment.

25TH.—Remained in camp.

26TH.—Column extended along the blockhouse line to strengthen it during a drive from north to south, Pretoria --Koomati Poort railway line to Standerton—Elansfontein line. Regiment took up line with right on Onverwacht, left on Langsluit.

Half a squadron of the regiment became engaged with the Manchester Regiment on the left of the driving line, the two forces firing at each other for about half-an-hour before the mistake was discovered. No. 4454, Private J. Woodward was seriously wounded, and No. 3053, Private Hillier, 15th Hussars, attached, was also wounded. No. 4758, Private W. Galloway wounded at Vlaklaagte.

27TH.—Marched to Langverwacht, where the regiment concentrated.

APRIL, 1902.

28TH.—Marched into Vaal. The column concentrated here.

Lieutenant C. E. Soames and the following draft left Queenstown and disembarked at Capetown on the 18th April, 1902, and joined the regiment at Vaal, and were posted to squadrons as follows:—

"A" Squadron.

5063 S.S. J. Gillies.	4167 Pte. E. Lumley.
3845 Tptr. H. Dove.	3145 Pte. W. Parrott.
5319 Pte. P. Britten.	3148 Pte. A. Strange.
5324 Pte. A. Dwyer.	2978 Pte. G. Tilley.
5266 Pte. T. James.	

"B" Squadron

4645 Sergt. W. Hawke.	4758 Pte. W. Galloway.
3534 Sergt.-Farr. C. Bolton.	5274 Pte. J. Kelly.
3075 S.S. E. Kelligan.	3380 Pte. J. Morgan.
4461 Tptr. H. Pearce.	5094 Pte. W. Morrison.
4342 Pte. P. Armour.	5275 Pte. J. Regan.
4765 Pte. T. Coltman.	3023 Pte. E. Watters.

"C" Squadron.

2904 Cpl.-Sadlr. A. Vanstan.	3821 Pte. G. Hart.
3515 S.S. J. Clery.	4366 Pte. W. James.
4680 Pte. E. Arneil.	3452 Pte. W. G. Lawson.
4369 Pte. R. Cooper.	2928 Pte. W. Nelville.
3823 Pte. W. Hogg.	3535 Pte. J. Murphy.
4878 Pte. J. Hanna.	

1ST MAY.—The last two days were spent in camp at Vaal. To-day we marched at mid-day to Goodgedacht.

2ND.—Started on drive to Vrede—Frankfort—Heilbron blockhouse line. Convoy failed to get up with the column, and the troops got no food on reaching camp.

About 60 Boers broke through the driving line, wounding No. 3316, Private Proctor.

3RD.—Continued the drive to the blockhouse line. Result, 87 prisoners.

5TH.—Marched at 3 p.m. to Frischgewaagd, where orders were received to take four days' rations and forage on man and horse. No wheeled transport of any kind

MAY, 1902.
allowed to accompany the troops on the coming drive, which was on to the Lindley—Kroonstrad blockhouse line. Column Commanders:—Rimington, Lawley, Spens, Nixon, Garrett, McKenzie, Duff, Allenby, Little, Fanshawe.

6TH.—Started at 5.30 a.m. Convoy and guns returned to Frankfort. Soon after the drive started Boers were seen moving about in an excitable manner in front of the line. The 19th Hussars were working on our right, and Colonel Allenby's Column on our left. " C " Squadron captured nine Boers and remained for a time with Colonel Fanshawe's Column. " A " and " B " Squadrons arrived at Groenvlei, near Lindley, after a march of about 60 miles, and bivouacked next to Little's Column (14th Hussars, King's Dragoon Guards, and 7th Dragoon Guards). Result of the drive, 26 Boers killed, 226 prisoners; about 250 broke through Colonel McKenzie's Column.

7TH.—Colonel Little's Column left. " C " Squadron rejoined.

8TH.—Formed up for drive back to Frankfort—Heilbron blockhouse line. Regiment on right of the column.

9TH.—Started at 5 a.m. on the drive, Colonel Allenby's Column on our right and 19th Hussars Regiment on our left. Saw no Boers. All our advanced screen got too far to the left, and consequently became engaged with Colonel McKenzie's Column, No. 4366, Private C. Anderson being wounded.

It was dark before the drive ended, and the column concentrated at Vlakplaats and bivouacked there. Result of the drive, 28 prisoners. Two-hundred Boers broke through Colonel Spens' Column.

10TH.—Marched to Deelfontein, where we found the convoy and the camp ready pitched.

11TH.—Remained in camp.

12TH.—Marched to Wolverpoort.

MAY, 1902.

13TH.—Marched to Zandfontein. Column extended and parties told off to burn the grass veldt.

14TH.—Marched to Vlakfontein.

15TH.—Marched to Greylingstad.

18TH.—Remained at Greylingstad until to-day, when we moved to Vlakfontein and joined Colonel McKenzie's Column.

20TH.—No. 4687, Pte. F. Hatton died at Charlestown of enteric fever.

1ST JUNE.—News received of the Declaration of Peace. Great rejoicing.

28TH.—No. 2996, Private H. McIlvenny died at Standerton of dysentery.

29TH.—No. 4194, Private F. Gavin died at Standerton of enteric fever.

DIARY OF "C" SQUADRON AND A DETACHMENT OF "A" SQUADRON, 19TH FEBRUARY, 1902 to 24TH APRIL, 1902.

19TH FEBRUARY, 1902.—Ninety non-commissioned officers of "A" Squadron left Volksrust for Botha's Pass under Captain Jennings and Lieutenant Lomer.

20TH.—Men lined out in the trenches between Quagga Nek and Botha's Pass.

23RD.—Men collected from trenches to Botha's Pass and marched to Klip River Post to join remainder of "A" Squadron and Colonel Nixon's Column. "A" Squadron officers, Captain P. M. Jennings, Lieutenant C. J. M. Lomer, and Second-Lieutenant J. C. Brutton.

24TH.—Column marched to Boschfontein, and was joined during the day by "C" Squadron from Cork Farm. "C" Squadron officers, Major J. A. Henderson, Lieutenant J. Van der Byl, Second-Lieutenant Hon. R. N. D. Ryder.

25TH.—"C" Squadron and part of "A" Squadron attacked at 11.30 p.m. Boers repulsed. (Our casualties one man killed and four wounded; see "C" Squadron

SOUTH AFRICAN WAR

FEBRUARY, 1902.

Diary). "A" Squadron killed two and wounded two Boers about three yards from camp.

26TH.—The drive ended to-day; camped near Albertina.

3RD MARCH.—Lieutenant Holford joined "A" Squadron and Captain Threlfall "C" Squadron.

4TH.—Left Albertina on another drive. For particulars of this drive see "C" Squadron Diary from this date to the 12th, when the drive ended near Roodevaal Station.

15TH.—Moved to Vredefort Road Station. "A" and "C" Squadrons, with two squadrons of the 20th Hussars, moved out under Major Henderson to Leeuwspruit to guard the line.

17TH.—Returned to Vredefort Road Station.

19TH.—Drive commenced (particulars of this drive will be found in the Diary of "C" Squadron).

24TH.—Joined the regiment with Colonel Wing's Column.

SAMPLES OF SIGNALLING MESSAGES ON SERVICE.

The following is a copy of a lamp message received to-night:—

Begins :—" General French.

Am four miles west of Dewetsdorp, enemy holding a strong line facing West and South-west five or six miles long, strongly entrenched covering Dewetsdorp. They have five or six guns, and their force is variously estimated at from six thousand (stop). Please helio to me your opinion tomorrow." Ends.

Helio Message.

General French

Begins :—" One Squadron due East reports all clear. One patrol that went round North-east of the mountain has just returned being heavily fired on from kopjes N.E. ; a Squadron is now being sent towards Alexandriesfontein again. Our first officer's patrol to that place has not returned or sent in information."
G.O.C. Cav. Dlv. Ends.

Helio Message.

Gen. Hamilton

Begins :—" Large party of Boers and laager seen trekking towards us from N. end of mountain. We shelled and turned them back to mountain—Have sent two Squadrons forward to try to intercept—can spare no more—can you send M.I.

General Dickson." Ends.

The following is a true copy of a Boer " Summary of News."

Official Telegram.

From	To
General Telegraph Office, Pretoria.	Telegraph Office, Ermelo.

Pretoria, 24th May, 1900.

Orange Free State :—23/5/00.

Yesterday afternoon our Burghers had a fight with the enemy near Heilbron and our Burghers had to retire as the enemy were in too large numbers. The enemy went into Heilbron yesterday at 10 a.m. The Burghers retired to the left of Vredefort.

On May 22nd, the town of Lindley was re-occupied by Prinsloo, and the line of communication with Bethlehem was re-established. In the fight with the enemy near Lindley, 60 of the enemy were killed or wounded and 20 taken prisoners ; three officers were taken. The prisoners have just arrived at Pretoria.

A big column of the enemy about 3000 strong with 10 cannons and a few Maxims are going up to Vredefort.

Natal Borders :—

Information from the English Doctor—Dr. Nicholson. According to the identification cards, 105 killed and wounded were lost in the fight of the 20th of May, at Scheepers Nek. Among the killed there is a Captain, two Lieutenants, and a few N.C.O's. The enemy were about 300 or 400 strong with 2 cannon. It was too dark to follow the enemy at the conclusion of the fight.

Pretoria, 25th of May.

Vaal River,
    24th May.

The enemy are trekking along the Vaal.

Orange Free State :—

A report has come in that Vredefort is occupied by the enemy, and later that the enemy are advancing towards Schoemans Drift. Later report from Commandant De Wet states that the Burghers have retaken Heilbron.

Potchefstroom :—

A report states that Burghers came in freely to the Commando, and a lot of Boer women brought their sons who are under 17 years of age to the Commandant, and ordered them to fight to the bitter end.

From	To
General Smutz,	Landrost,
Vereeniging,	Ermelo.
24/5/00.	

A conference among Officers has decided that all cattle belonging to Burghers who refuse to fight shall be confiscated; their live stock shall be divided among the Commandos in the Field.
' This shall be published.

DIARY "C" SQUADRON.

27TH MAY, 1901.—Major Henderson, Second-Lieutenant Woods and Headquarters "C" Squadron left Volksrust by train at noon. Arrived at Glencoe at 6 p.m., and bivouacked there.

28TH.—Started from Glencoe at 8.30 a.m. and marched to Dundee. Encamped on north side of town.

30TH.—Marched from Dundee as portion of escort to a convoy of 112 wagons. The force, under command of Lieutenant-Colonel Lambart, Royal Artillery, encamped on east side of Buffalo River at De Jager's Drift.

31ST.—Formed left flank guard of convoy and marched to Blood River. Bivouacked there.

1ST JUNE.—Marched at 6.45 a.m. and arrived at Vryheid at 2 p.m.

2ND.—Small escort went out with party to fetch coal, and saw a few Boers near Holbane.

3RD.—Marched from Vryheid at 6.45 a.m. Formed right flank guard to convoy. Bivouacked at Blood River.

JUNE, 1901.

4TH.—Marched from Blood River at 6.45 a.m. Bivouacked at De Jager's Drift.

5TH.—Marched into Dundee.

9TH.—Marched from Dundee at 7.25 a.m. Formed portion of escort to convoy force under command of Lieutenant-Colonel Matthews, Royal Lancaster Regiment. Bivouacked at De Jager's Drift.

11TH.—Marched from De Jager's Drift at 7.25 a.m. Bivouacked at Blood River.

12TH.—Marched from Blood River 7.30 a.m. The 12-pounder fired a few shells at distant Boers at Scheeper's Nek. Bivouacked Vryheid.

13TH.—Marched from Vryheid at 8 a.m. Rear Guard fired a few shells in the neighbourhood of Scheeper's Nek. Bivouacked Rooi Kopjes.

14TH.—Marched from Rooi Kopjes at 7.30 a.m. Bivouacked at De Jager's Drift.

15TH.—Left De Jager's Drift at 8 a.m. and marched into Dundee.

24TH.—Remainder of " C " Squadron (103 men and 87 horses), under Second-Lieutenant Ryder, arrived at Dundee from Volksrust.

25TH.—Detachments of " B " Squadron which had been attached to " C " Squadron on May 27th, returned to Volksrust. Second-Lieutenant Woods remained in Dundee.

Moved camp to new site south of town.

29TH.—Detachments of 40 men, under Lieutenant Woods, marched at 9 a.m. for One Tree Hill.

3RD JULY.—Patrol of 30 men sent out at 8.30 p.m. in the direction of Waschbank.

4TH.—Patrols sent to Indumeni and towards Helpmakaar. All these patrols returned without seeing anything.

5TH.—Detachment under Lieutenant Woods returned from One Tree Hill.

SOUTH AFRICAN WAR

JULY, 1901.

6TH.—Detachment under Lieutenant Woods left Helpmakaar. Patrol went to Gregory's Nek.

10TH.—Patrol under Sergeant Fosdyke started for Waschbank and Helpmakaar.

11TH.—A small escort sent towards Nqutu and a night patrol to Gregory's Nek.

12TH.—Sergeant Fosdyke's patrol returned without result. Supplies sent to Helpmakaar.

15TH.—Detachments of 21 men and horses left by train to join the detachment at Upper Tugela.

16TH.—Various small patrols sent out.

19TH.—Sergeant Walsh arrived with party of "C" Squadron from Newcastle.

Three strong patrols sent out.

22ND.—A small party arrived from Volksrust to join squadron.

23RD.—Squadron made reconnaissance towards Waschbank.

25TH.—The squadron, with two guns 67th Battery and 20 Mounted Infantry, formed a force under Major Henderson. Left Dundee at 4 p.m. Joined by 10 men V.C.R. at Malnngeni. Reached Laffney's Drift at 10 p.m. and bivouacked there. Strength of squadron on this occasion was 85.

26TH.—Columns started at 6.45 a.m., and reconnoitred round Vetch Kop and Kopje Alleen. Major Jeros Edwards' force joined the column at 1 p.m. Bivouacked south side of Nkausa.

27TH.—Column started at 5.30 a.m. Marched to Munkea. Bivouacked in concealment during day. Two Boers were captured by outposts.

Column marched again at 9 p.m.

28TH.—The transport, ambulance, etc., were left in entrenched position at Halte Beeste Laagte, with a guard, under command of Captain R. Parker, Lancaster

K

JULY, 1901.

Regiment. Remainder of column, consisting of 70 8th Hussars, 85 V.R.C., and one gun, under Major Henderson, continued march at 1 a.m. Arrived at Commandant Grobelar's Farm, Beward, at 7.30 a.m. Captured two Boers. Grobelar escaped. At 9.15 a.m. Boers attacked in force. Columns commenced retirement towards Nondweni. Fought successive rear guard actions to the drift, and finally took up position on west side of river, being practically surrounded by the enemy. The attack continued heavy until 5 p.m., when it was finally repulsed and Boers retired. Column continued its march to Woolmore's Store, Nondweni, and bivouacked there at 7.30 p.m.

8th Hussars' casualties:—No. 2997, Sergeant Fosdyke, killed.

No. 4038, Private Wheaton, and 4434, Private Wright, severely wounded.

No. 4991, Private F. McCarthy, and 5271, Private W. Waller, missing, afterwards rejoined.

(Major Henderson and Squadron-Sergeant-Major Burns mentioned in despatches).

29TH.—Remainder of column re-joined at Nondweni at 6.30 a.m. Column marched at 7 a.m. and arrived at Nqutu 3 p.m. Bivouacked there.

30TH.—Sergeant Fosdyke and five others buried to-day at mid-day.

Column broke up.

2ND AUGUST.—Squadron marched at 9 a.m. with the Boer prisoners. Arrived at Vant's Drift at 3 p.m. and bivouacked there.

3RD.—Squadron marched at 7 a.m. Arrived at Dundee at 2 p.m.

8TH.—A small detachment, under Corporal Parrott, sent to De Waal's Farm.

10TH.—Squadron marched at 12.30 p.m. Arrived at De Jager's Drift at 4.30 p.m.

SOUTH AFRICAN WAR

AUGUST, 1901.

13TH.—Left De Jager's Drift at 1 p.m. Arrived at Dundee 4.30 p.m.

17TH.—The detachment under Lieutenant Van der Byl from Upper Tugela, arrived and rejoined the squadron.

18TH.—Marched at 7.30 a.m., part of escort to convoy under command of Major Henderson. Bivouacked at Dè Jager's Drift.

19TH.—Squadron joined column under command of Colonel Blomfield. Marched at 8 a.m. 8th Hussars left flank and rear guard. Bivouacked on east of Blood River.

20TH.—Marched at 8 a.m. Johannesburg Mounted Rifles shelled a few distant Boers from Scheeper's Nek. Arrived Vryheid 5 p.m. Bivouacked on show ground.

22ND.—Reconnaissance east of Vryheid, searching farms and bringing in families. Rear guard action on return march. Private Gaisford wounded at 2,400 yards.

23RD.—Reconnaissance towards Kambala Draai. Returned to Vryheid at 3 p.m.

24TH.—Colonel Pulteney's force joined the column.

27TH.—Column under Colonel Blomfield marched at 7 a.m. Some fighting near Hlobane. Bivouacked at Rietolei.

28TH.—Marched by Waterval (L. Botha's Farm) to Goudhoek. No Boers.

29TH.—Reconnaissance to Dipka, near the Pivaan. Boers retired.

30TH.—Column marched at 7.30 a.m. A good deal of fighting with the Scheltks Commando on left flank. Bivouacked at Nooitgedacht. Picquets attacked at night and camp fired into. Two of the 8th Hussars hit.

31ST.—Column marched into Vryheid at 1 p.m. Rear guard had some fighting.

2ND SEPTEMBER.—Column marched at 6.30 a.m. in south easterly direction, sniping during the day and at night. Bivouacked at Groenkop.

DIARY OF THE

SEPTEMBER, 1901.

3RD.—Continued march by Tabankula. Rear guard actions. Bivouacked at Brakfontein.

4TH.—Squadron in camp. Raided neighbouring farms.

5TH.—Column marched to Nondweni.

6TH.—Portion of column and 8th Hussars, under Major Henderson, marched to Vant's Drift and bivouacked there.

7TH.—Marched at 7 a.m. Arrived at Dundee 2 p.m

8TH.—Detachment from Besters, under Lieutenant Threlfall, arrived at Dundee and re-joined the squadron.

10TH.—Squadron marched from Dundee to form portion of an escort to convoy under command of Colonel Matthews, Royal Lancaster Regiment. Bivouacked at De Jager's Drift.

12TH.—Marched 7 a.m. 8th Hussars on left flank. Bivouacked at Blood River.

13TH.—Marched 7 a.m. Arrived Vryheid 1.30 p.m.

17TH.—Reconnaissance towards Schuroeberg under Colonel Matthews, to support Colonel Gough's advance towards Vryheid. A corporal of the V.R.C. killed by lightning.

19TH.—Squadron employed in strengthening the defences of Vryheid. Preparations made for occupation of trenches, etc.

28TH.—Marched at 6 a.m. Bivouacked at Rooi Kopjes.

30TH.—Marched back with escort under Colonel Matthews and bivouacked at Rooi Kopjes.

1ST OCTOBER.—Marched at 5 a.m. Bivouacked at De Jager's Drift. Several of our horses died from tulip poisoning.

2ND.—Marched at 9 a.m. with Colonel Moody and Royal Irish Fusiliers. Bivouacked at Rooi Kopjes.

3RD.—Escorted detachment Royal Irish Fusiliers to Scheeper's Nek and brought back empty convoy to Rooi Kopjes.

OCTOBER, 1901.

4TH.—Marched at 5 a.m. as escort to empty convoy. Bivouacked at De Jager's Drift.
5TH.—Marched at 6 a.m. as escort to 150 wagons. Bivouacked under Rooi Kop.
6TH.—Marched at 5 a.m. Arrived at 5 p.m. at Vryheid with convoy.
7TH.—Marched as escort to wagons. Bivouacked under Rooi Kop.
8TH.—Marched at 7 a.m. and arrived at De Jager's Drift at 4.30 p.m. A good deal of fighting took place during the night.
9TH.—Communicated with Squadron Depot which had remained at Dundee under Lieutenant Ryder.
12TH.—Marched at 3 p.m. Arrived at De Jager's Drift at 8 p.m.
14TH.—Squadron marched to Uys Kop and brought back empty convoy.
15TH.—Escorted convoy to Uys Kop and brought back empty wagons.
16TH.—Escorted convoy to Uys Kop and brought back empty wagons.
20TH.—Escorted large convoy as far as Uys Kop and returned.
22ND.—One troop on escort duty.
24TH.—Marched at 5 a.m. as escort to convoy of 60 wagons. Returned from Uys Kop with empty wagons.
26TH.—Escorted convoy to Uys Kop and returned.
27TH.—Escorted 107 wagons to Uys Kop and brought empty convoy.
29TH.—Escorted small convoy to Uys Kop and returned.
30TH.—Two troops went out and brought empty convoy. Private Dawson, riding from Dundee, was drowned by the floods at Zandspruit.
31ST.—Escorted convoy to Uys Kop and returned.
1ST NOVEMBER.—Escorted convoy to Uys Kop and returned.

NOVEMBER, 1901.

2ND.—Two troops, under Captain Van der Byl, went out and brought in empty convoy.

6TH.—Started from De Jager's Drift with convoy at 5 a.m. Bivouacked at Rooi Kopjes.

7TH.—Marched at 5 a.m. Arrived at Vryheid at 4 p.m. Met a squadron of the regiment there under Captain Mussenden.

9TH.—Marched at 5 a.m. with an empty convoy of 250 wagons. Bivouacked at Rooi Kopjes.

10TH.—Marched at 5.30 a.m. Arrived at De Jager's Drift at 3 p.m.

12TH.—No. 4870, Private Rearden drowned on the Buffalo River, which was in flood at the time.

13TH.—Escorted convoy and took out some Australian details to Colonel Pulteney's and Colonel Garrett's Columns. Bivouacked at Rooi Kopjes and found Captain Mussenden's Squadron there.

14TH.—Marched at 5 a.m. and arrived at Vryheid at 4 p.m.

15TH.—Marched at 5.45 a.m. and bivouacked at Rooi Kopjes.

16TH.—Marched at 6 a.m. and arrived at De Jager's Drift at 3 p.m.

19TH.—Marched at 6 a.m. with convoy under Colonel Porter, New Zealand. Bivouacked at Rooi Kopjes.

21ST.—Captain Threlfall took one troop to Lucas Meyer's farm to collect wood.

22ND.—Marched at 6 a.m. Bivouacked at Rooi Kopjes.

23RD.—Marched at 6 a.m. Arrived at De Jager's Drift at 2 p.m.

24TH.—Three troops, under Major Henderson, marched into Dundee. One troop, under Sergeant Wilkes, remaining at De Jager's Drift.

30TH.—Detachment under Captain Threlfall proceeded to Helpmakaar in relief of Lieutenant Woods'

SOUTH AFRICAN WAR

NOVEMBER, 1901.

detachment, which had been there since July 6th. Major Henderson accompanied the party.

1ST DECEMBER.—Squadron received orders to find ten entrenchments in the Dundee Sub-District in relief of the V.C.R.

2ND.—The various detachments marched from Dundee. Lieutenant Woods went in command to De Jager's Drift, Second-Lieutenant Ryder to Slangberg.

4TH.—Major Henderson proceeded to Volksrust to take over temporary command of the regiment. The headquarters of "C" Squadron remained at Dundee under Captain Van der Byl.

12TH.—"C" Squadron ordered to concentrate at Dundee for a trek to Zululand. Major Henderson and Lieutenant Curell re-joined at Dundee.

14TH.—"C" Squadron joined column under Lieutenant-Colonel Evans, V.C.R. Marched at 9 a.m. and bivouacked at Rorke's Drift.

15TH.—Marched into Zululand and bivouacked about eight miles east of Isandhlwana.

16TH.—Marched at 5 a.m. Sniping from Boers near Louisfort. Bivouacked under Babanango.

17TH.—Our force joined column under Lieutenant-Colonel Chapman, R.D.F., and bivouacked on plateau of Babanango.

18TH.—Reconnaissance and occupation of Babanango and Scheeper's Hoek; 8th Hussars in advance. Boers evacuated their positions. Commenced night march at 7 p.m.

19TH.—Arrived at Derdiend at 5 a.m. Thick mist and rain hindered operations.

20TH.—Marched at 4 a.m. Arrived at Entonjaneni at 7 a.m.

26TH.—Marched from Entonjaneni, viâ Prospect. Bivouacked at Cooper's Store, near the Umplatusi.

27TH. — Marched by Itala to Uhlelu ridge and bivouacked there.

DECEMBER, 1901.

28TH.—Squadron and some Mounted Infantry detached on right flank. Heavy sniping on Babanango, but no casualties. Bivouacked north-west of Fort Louis.

29TH.—Marched to Nondweni. Sniping en route among Maawuglni Hills.

31ST.—Marched by Nqutu to Vant's Drift.

1ST JANUARY, 1902.—Marched at 4.30 a.m. Arrived at Dundee at 10 a.m.

3RD.—Main body of squadron marched at 7 a.m., Lieutenant Curell remaining in charge of Squadron Depôt at Dundee, and Sergeant Wilkes and detachment remaining at De Jager's Drift. Bivouacked at Daunhauser.

4TH.—Marched at 5 a.m. and arrived at Newcastle at 1 p.m.

5TH.—General Burn Murdoch complimented squadron on the condition of their horses.

6TH.—Marched at 5 a.m. and escorted convoy to Botha's Post.

7TH.—Marched at 6 a.m. and bivouacked at Botha's Pass.

8TH.—Marched at 7 a.m. along blockhouse line. Bivouacked at Rorinek.

9TH.—Marched to Cork Farm. Found General Bullock and Colonel Garrett there, also a squadron 8th Hussars, under Captain Lord Garnock.

10TH.—" C " Squadron joined General Bullock's Column.

11TH.—Marched at 12.30 a.m. with Q.I.B., under Colonel H. White. Saw 40 or 50 Boers. One captured. Returned to camp.

12TH.—Squadron employed in strengthening post at Cork Farm.

13TH.—8th Hussars, under Major Henderson, made reconnaissance northwards. Attacked by about 400 Boers. Took up a position and held it until Colonel Garrett's appearance in the distance caused enemy to retire. The following were the list of casualties:—

SOUTH AFRICAN WAR 137

JANUARY, 1902.
No. 4714, Private J. Balls, No. 5115, Private J. Brandford, No. 4261, Private W. Mann, and No. 4679, Private W. Fitzgerald, killed in action, Welkomsfontein.
Lieutenant C. M. Threlfall, gun-shot wound, leg, slight.
Second-Lieutenant H. St. L. Malet, gun-shot wound, shoulder and arm, severe.
No. 5069, Private W. Aldridge, severely wounded.
No. 4712, Private H. Bintcliffe, severe.
No. 3369, Private H. H. Hayes, slight.
No. 3377, Private J. Legood, slight.
No. 3576, Private G. Sugars, dangerous.
No. 5001, Private Uckermann, severe.
No. 2705, Private E. J. Stone, 15th Hussars, attached, slight.

15TH.—Squadron employed under General Bullock in covering the construction of the blockhouse line. Made small reconnaissance.

18TH.—Portion of "B" Squadron, 8th Hussars, under Captain Mort, arrived.

19TH.—Night alarm and heavy firing at Cork Farm and along blockhouse line.

24TH.—Column marched at 4.30 a.m. and bivouacked at Wilgenbad.
No. 5165, Private C. Bullen, died at Charlestown Hospital of enteric fever.

27TH.—Marched to Tweekopjes and joined forces with General E. O. Hamilton.

31ST.—Marched back to Cork Farm. "B" Squadron, under Captain Mort, left the column and went on to Witkopjes.

1ST FEBRUARY. — Captain Van der Byl carried out a small reconnaissance in a south-east direction, but saw nothing of enemy.

2ND.—Captain Lord Garnock commanded party to cover Reynolds' Scouts, collecting cattle and horses.

3RD.—Marched at 6 a.m. and bivouacked at Klip River. One troop of "A" Squadron went on to Botha's Pass.

FEBRUARY, 1902.

5TH.—Marched back to Cork Farm. Remainder of "A" Squadron, under Captain Lord Garnock, went to Botha's Pass.

7TH.—Captain Van der Byl took out a party to cover Reynolds' Scouts, who were being driven back to camp. No casualties.

8TH.—Reconnoitring patrol went out under Second-Lieutenant Ryder.

10TH.—Reconnoitring patrol out under Captain Van der Byl. Night alarm. Boers endeavouring to cross blockhouse line.

15TH.—Various reconnoitring patrols sent out from Cork Farm daily.

20TH.—Squadron employed in digging and occupying trenches to re-inforce the blockhouse line.

21ST.—Squadron distributed in the trenches along the blockhouse line.

23RD.—Squadron collected from the trenches and marched to Witkopjes.

24TH.—Marched at 4 a.m. and joined Colonel Nixon's Column. "A" Squadron of the regiment already there under Captain Jennings.

25TH.—Column marched at 6 a.m. through the Witkopjes and bivouacked on Sterkfontein. "C" Squadron on outpost.

26TH.—Large force of Boers made a determined attempt to break through the line at Sterkfontein at 12.30 a.m. Brunt of the attack fell on Sergeant Champion's picquet, who succeeded in driving them off with the following casualties:—

No. 4110, Private A. Tubby, killed.
No. 4663, Private C. Spencer, wounded (dangerous).
No. 4920, Private E. Kent, wounded.
No. 3481, Private Kirwan, wounded (dangerous).
No. 4380, Private E. Street, wounded.

Later we marched across the Mill River to Gelderland. "C" Squadron killed two Boers and captured ten.

FEBRUARY, 1902.

27TH.—Marched to within four miles of Albertina. This drive was very successful. The number of Boers accounted for by "C" Squadron was 3 killed, 3 wounded, and 18 unwounded prisoners.

28TH.—Marched to Albertina and encamped there. The total captures in this drive amounted to over 700 Boers, most of whom surrendered in a body to Colonel Rawlinson. The total of Colonel Nixon's Column was 76 Boers.

3RD MARCH.—Lieut. Holford joined "A" Squadron.

4TH.—Marched at 8 a.m., preparatory to another drive. Went by north side of Plat Berg to Glen Paul, and bivouacked there. In these drives Colonel Nixon's Column always maintained the same formation: 3rd Hussars on the right; 20th Hussars on the left; 8th Hussars in the centre.

5TH.—Marched at 6.30 a.m. and took up a line from Hardyville to Majoors Drift, over the Wilge River.

6TH.—Marched at 6.30 a.m. and took up a line from Vinksnest to Rust.

7TH.—The line advanced to Orma.

8TH.—The column advanced and took up a line from Zamenkorust to Leeuw Kop.

9TH.—Column advanced to Kromspruit and Barnkiss.

10TH.—Column made a 35 miles march to Cyphergat and Morgendal.

11TH.—Made another long march and bivouacked on south bank of Rhenoster Spruit, near Kopje Aleen.

12TH.—Column marched at 11 a.m., crossed river, and bivouacked Roodeval.

15TH.—Column marched at 8 a.m. and encamped near Vredefort Road Station. 8th Hussars, with two squadrons 20th Hussars, under Major Henderson, marched again at 7 p.m. Bivouacked at Leeuwspruit.

16TH.—Made reconnaissance along north bank of the Rhenoster and returned to bivouac.

17TH.—Re-joined column at Vredefort Road.

19TH.—Column marched to Walfontein.

MARCH, 1902.

20TH.—Marched at 7 a.m. and took up place in the driving line from Bosch Kopjes to Vredeverway—Colonel Garrett on the left, Colonel Barker on the right.

21ST.—Column advanced to Baviaankrann and Mount Prospect.

22ND.—Advanced to Omdraai Nord and Riidebloem. Found three Krupp guns buried.

23RD.—Marched to Liebensberg Vlei and took up line along east bank.

25TH.—Crossed river and bivouacked on opposite bank.

26TH.—Marched at 7 a.m. and advanced to the Wilge River, which was in flood.

1ST APRIL.—The line was detained until now by the height of the flood. Column crossed river and took up a line two miles east of it near Bamboes Spruit.

2ND.—Column advanced at 6.45 a.m. along course of Hol Spruit. Drove back number of Boers near Kalk Kran. Trumpeter Proctor wounded.

3RD.—Advanced to Mill River. Saw a good many Boers.

4TH.—One squadron, with a pom-pom went back, under Major Henderson, to reinforce rear-guard of 20th Hussars who had been attacked. Column advanced four miles up Mill River.

5TH.—Advanced to the Drakenberg and took up line from Normandien to Muller's Pass.

6TH.—Searched various kloofs on the Drakenberg.

7TH.—Canadians fired into our camp by mistake, with the result that No. 5277, Private G. Griffiths, was killed.

8TH.—8th Hussars moved into camp with headquarters of column close to Muller's Pass.

9TH.—Column marched at 7 a.m. to Klip River post on blockhouse line.

10TH.—Marched along blockhouse line and bivouacked near Hout Hoek.

11TH.—Column reconnoitred the country between Witkopjes and the blockhouse line. Bivouacked between Cork Farm and Wagen Pad.

12TH.—8th Hussars reconnoitred the hills north of Wagen Pad. Re-joined column near Vrede. Bivouacked at Geluk.

13TH.—Marched 6.30 a.m. Rear guard of 3rd Hussars attacked during mid-day out-span. Crossed Vaal at Roberts' Drift and bivouacked on north bank.

14TH.—Started at 6.30 a.m. and made a long march to Greylingstad.

17TH.—Marched at 7 a.m. north-west from Greylingstad into position for another drive.

18TH.—Advanced about 16 miles and bivouacked near Bushman's Kop.

19TH.—Marched at 6.30 a.m. and advanced about 17 miles. Bivouacked with our right flank on Wilge.

20TH.—Started at 5.30 a.m. Marched about 30 miles. No Boers seen. Bivouacked 4 miles south-west of Bragspruit Station.

22ND.—8th Hussars left Colonel Nixon's Column. Marched at 6.45 a.m. to Steenkoolspruit and bivouacked near South African Constabulary post.

23RD.—Marched at 7 a.m. along South African Constabulary blockhouse line to Onvervacht, and bivouacked there.

DIARY OF "B" SQUADRON WITH COLONEL PULTENEY'S COLUMN.

15TH SEPTEMBER, 1901.—Marched to Lang Kloof, arriving at 5 p.m. Very wet and windy.

16TH.—Convoy arrived and we marched to Schurve Kop and bivouacked.

17TH.—The column started at 7 a.m., but we did not leave until 10 a.m. as rear guard. Marched to Beacon Hill Fort and off-saddled, waiting for the wagons. Started at 2 p.m. and scrambled down the steep pass to

SEPTEMBER, 1901.
the foot of North Hill, which we reached at 6 p.m. and bivouacked in a thunderstorm.

18TH.—Started at 7 a.m. and marched down mountain pass to Utrecht, where we off-saddled. Started again at 1 p.m. and marched to Stales Drift, over the Buffalo River, where we bivouacked and were joined by Major King, Royal Artillery, one squadron 14th Hussars under Jameson, 80 Dublin Mounted Infantry, and two field guns.

20TH.—Paraded at 4.30 a.m., but did not start till 5.30, as it was too dark until then. Marched to Cattle Drift and bivouacked.

21ST.—Convoy went to Newcastle for stores, under command of Lieutenant Partridge.

Lieutenant Allen took a patrol to the Stales and Inchanga Drifts.

22ND.—Convoy returned.

23RD.—Started at 6.30 a.m. and marched to Dundee.

24TH.—The 5th Dragoon Guards and 13th Hussars arrived with Colonel Hamilton.

25TH.—Marched at 7 a.m. to De Jager's Drift.

27TH.—We should have marched at 7 a.m. for Vryheid, but at the last minute these orders were cancelled and we re-crossed the Drift and filled up the wagons, marching at 11.30 a.m. to Robson's Farm.

28TH.—Started at 6.15 a.m. as rear guard, to Vant's Drift. Took three days' supplies there and went on without wagons to Umblambambosa, where we bivouacked at 6 p.m. Very rough country. Passed close to Rorkes Drift and Isandhlwana.

29TH.—Marched at 6 a.m. and bivouacked at Fort Lewis. The squadron was on outpost to-night, as an attack was expected.

Gen. Bruce Hamilton's Column camped 5 miles east of us.

1ST OCTOBER.—A sudden order was received at 2 p.m. to march at once; started and acted as right flank guard

SOUTH AFRICAN WAR

OCTOBER, 1901.

to Umbundase River, which we reached at 6 p.m. Bivouacked.

2ND.—The column was ordered to march at 6 a.m., but owing to the mist it was not possible to make a start until 8.30 a.m. Squadron acted as advance guard to Nqutu in Zululand, where we arrived at noon and bivouacked.

4TH.—Marched as right flank guard to convoy to Nondweni, where we bivouacked at 7 a.m.

5TH.—Marched to Spitz Kop, where we bivouacked at 3 p.m.

6TH.—Marched as advance guard to Bethel, which we reached at 10 a.m. and bivouacked.

7TH.—Column convoy went to Vryheid for supplies.

10TH.—Marched at 5.30 a.m. and bivouacked at Brakfontein about 5 p.m. Acted as rear guard to column.

11TH. Started at 6 a.m. as right flank guard to Vryheid. Off-saddled and got supplies and then marched on to Scheeper's Nek, where we bivouacked at 5.30 p.m. in pouring rain, which continued all night.

12TH.—Started at 7.30 a.m. and marched towards De Jager's Drift. Off-saddled at Blood River, where we received orders to march to Utrecht. Moved off at 2 p.m. and marched to Grootvlei. Bivouacked at 4 p.m.

13TH.—Marched at 6 a.m. and arrived at Utrecht at 1 p.m. and bivouacked.

14TH.—Marched at 10 a.m. and bivouacked at Knight's Farm.

15TH.—Marched at 5.30 a.m. to Pivaan's Poort. Bivouacked at 4 p.m.

16TH.—Started at 6.30 a.m. and reached Zakiel's Nek about which the infantry beat the bush for a considerable distance with no result. Bivouacked at 6.30 p.m. at Koekraal Spruit.

17TH.—Started at 6.30 a.m. as advance guard to opposite the Pongola Bosch at Uitvlugt, where the Bosch was shelled and 300 head of cattle taken. The Boers then commenced sniping, and kept us there till dark. The

OCTOBER, 1901.

squadron held two kopjes on the north side of the Pongola River till the column passed and reached the camp at midnight. Bivouacked Chakas Spruit.

18TH.—Started at 8 a.m.—a pouring wet day—marched to Welbedacht, which place we reached at 11 a.m. and bivouacked, after acting as rear guard.

19TH.—Same camp; pouring wet day and very cold.

20TH.—Ordered to move at 11 a.m. as rear guard. Column moved off to Luneberg. The squadron was stopped and ordered to escort a convoy with Major Fell, Scottish Rifles, and one squadron 5th Dragoon Guards, under Colonel Eustace. Bivouacked at Chakas Spruit.

21ST.—Marched as advance guard and right flank guard to Diep Kloof.

22ND.—Started at 6 a.m. in a thick mist and bitterly cold weather, and on arriving at Knight's Farm, bivouacked.

23RD.—Started at 7 a.m. and marched as advance guard to Pivaans Poort, where we bivouacked. Very wet and cold.

24TH.—Started at 8 a.m. in thick mist, which cleared later, and marched as left flank guard to Chakas Spruit, arriving at 4 p.m.

25TH.—Started at 8 a.m. and marched to Welbedacht, joining Colonel Pulteney's Column again there.

26TH.—Started at 7 a.m. and marched to Uitvlugt, where we assisted in clearing the Pongola Bosch. Very thick bush and hard work.

27TH.—Started at 4 a.m. with Lieutenant Allen and 50 men and went with Colonel Pulteney and four companies of V.M.R. and one gun to Kaffir's Drift, and in conjunction with Colonel Plumer, cleared farms and searched bush round there. Got a lot of cattle and sheep and returned to camp at 5 p.m.

28TH.—Started at 8 a.m. as rear guard and marched to Chakas Spruit, where we bivouacked. Colonel Garrett's Column joined ours.

SOUTH AFRICAN WAR

OCTOBER, 1901.

29TH.—Started at 2 a.m. and marched with the squadron via Elandsberg Nek to Elands Nek, where we arrived at 5 a.m. and held two kopjes all day. Rejoined the column at Elandsberg at 6 p.m. Everyone wet through.

30TH.—Did not move all day owing to a thick fog. Rain all day.

31ST.—Started at 7 a.m. as right flank guard to convoy to One Tree Hill.

1ST NOVEMBER.—Same camp.

2ND.—Started at 9 a.m., marched to Spitz Kop and offsaddled for one hour, before marching to Schurveberg.

3RD.—Started at 6 a.m. and marched to Blood River Poort; halted at Blaauwstroom.

4TH.—Started at 8 a.m. Marched as rear guard. Bivouacked at Karnbuladraai.

5TH.—Started at 3 a.m. and marched to Nooitgedacht. Escort to guns. V.M.R. of our column met enemy. Killed two and took 12 prisoners, with a casualty list of one officer and two men killed and five wounded. Very wet day.

6TH.—Started at 5 a.m. and marched to Vryheid, where we remained until the 12th. " C " Squadron came in to the town on the 7th and left on the 9th.

12TH.—Small escort to Rooikopjes.

15TH.—Started at 5 a.m. and crawled to the top of Lancaster Hill and down to Gerust.

16TH.—Started at 4 a.m. Marched as advance guard to Pivaansbad Bridge, and thence to the north of Paul Pietersburg, where we camped. About 400 Boers bolted out of the town on our approach. Marched again at 10 p.m. to Jagt Drift, which was reached at 12.5 a.m. Held drift till convoy came up at 8 a.m. Marched again at 2 p.m. to Niederland, camping during a frightful thunderstorm.

18TH.—Started at 5.15 a.m. as rear guard to Anhalt.

NOVEMBER, 1901.

19TH.—Started at 6 a.m. and marched to Sturman's Ranges.

21ST.—Started at 3.30 a.m. and marched to Marienthal.

22ND.—Started at 7 a.m., acting as advance guard as far as No. 36 blockhouse at Annyspruit. Started again at 7 p.m. and marched all night.

23RD.—Left main body at Kaällwek at 12.5 a.m. and marched up steep pass to surround a farm, which was, however, drawn blank. Remained on the high ground all day, during which time we saw about 100 Boers in the valley some distance away being chased by Colonel Plumer's Column.

24TH.—Started at 5.15 a.m. to climb a steep pass over the Randbergen.

25TH.—Started at 6.30 a.m. and reached the top of the pass; about 10 a.m. marched on to Grootfontein and joined Colonel Plumer's Column.

26TH.—Started at 5 a.m., and after a long day's march, reached Rotterdam. Saw about 30 Boers during the day, and a little sniping took place.

27TH.—Started at 7 a.m. and marched to Lyden, and after pitching camp turned out to reconnoitre in the direction of Randbergen. Returned to camp at 3 p.m.

28TH.—Started at 12.15 a.m. and surrounded three farms before daylight, but caught no Boers. Continued the march, and camped at Brereton.

3RD DECEMBER.—We had remained in camp till to-day. Very wet weather has been experienced this last three or four days. Marched and camped at Kaalbank.

4TH.—Started at 5 a.m. and marched to Donkerhoek.

5TH.—Squadron-Quartermaster-Sergeant Hadler, with sick horses, started at 5 a.m. for Wakkerstroom and Volksrust. Our kits and spare wagons moved over to the Scottish Rifles' camp at 2 p.m. Started at 7 p.m., and marched all night. Carried three days' supplies.

6TH.—Saw about 200 Boers, but only long shots could be exchanged before they scooted.

DECEMBER, 1901.
7TH.—Marched at 3 a.m., and bivouacked at Mooipoort. Sergeant Mellish re-joined.
8TH.—Marched at 7 a.m. to Kleinfontein Nek, and returned to last night's camp at 3 p.m.
10TH.—Marched at 5 a.m. as rear guard to Amersfort.
11TH.—Started at 5 a.m. as advance guard to Piet Zyn Drift, from which about 100 Boers scooted on our approach, being immediately followed by the New Zealanders.
12TH.—Started at 5 a.m. and marched to Hartebeestfontein, capturing 3 prisoners and about 1,000 head of cattle on the way there.
13TH.—Started at 7.30 a.m. Marched as rear guard to Gras Kop. Wagons went in to Volksrust for supplies.
15TH.—Marched at 5 a.m. as right flank guard to Mooipoort, where bivouacked.
17TH.—Started at 10 a.m. Marched as far as Zoetfontein before bivouacking.
18TH.—Started at 5 a.m. Marched as right flank to Kalkoenskraal. Bivouacked at 11 a.m.
19TH.—Started at 1 a.m. and marched as advanced guard to top of hill, near Balmoral. Arrived there at 4 a.m. and off-saddled till 10 a.m. Camped at Balmoral, and whilst on Observation Post north of the camp was sniped by about 50 Boers, who were driven off. Started again at 11 p.m. and marched all night.

Had to halt from 1 a.m. till 4.30 a.m. owing to tremendous thunderstorms. When these ceased we marched to Rotterdam, where our guns shelled about 100 Boers, who trekked away in a north-east direction. A pouring wet day.
21ST.—Started at 7.30 a.m. The day was spent in signalling from Spitz Kop (which we reached about 10 a.m.) to General Bruce Hamilton.
22ND.—Marched back to Rotterdam and bivouacked.
23RD.—Started at 1 a.m. and marched to Balmoral, where we arrived at daybreak, and came across a lot of

DECEMBER, 1901.

Boers. Drove them to Voss Kop, where we arrived at noon. Could not get any further, as the horses were dead beaten. Fought all the way. Killed one, wounded one, and took six prisoners.

24TH.—Started at 4 a.m. and marched along the Randbergen. Saw nothing. Turned to the right at Spitz Kop and marched up to and across Elandsbergen and Naauwpoort, where bivouacked. Rear and flank guards sniped on reaching the high ground.

25TH.—Christmas Day. Moved our camp about a mile to the west.

28TH.—Started at 5 a.m. Marched as advanced guard to Vlackplaats (Amersfoort).

Lieutenant Partridge left in charge of an ox convoy proceeding to Wakkerstroom.

29TH.—Started at 1 a.m. and marched south-west until 4 a.m. Had to halt for fog until 8 a.m., when another move was made. Found about 150 Boers in front of us. Chased them to Kaffirs' kraal, and then drove them on to the blockhouse line and towards Colonel Spens' Column. Caught about 43. Camped at Skrydkraal at 7 p.m.

30TH.—Started at 5.30 a.m. Marched back to Naauwpoort, arriving at 7 p.m.

Private Flowerdew was badly kicked to-day about the face and head.

2ND JANUARY, 1902.—Started at 12.30 a.m. as advance guard to Spitz Kop, where we had to wait two hours for the fog to lift, then went to Balmoral, where we arrived at 4 p.m., and bivouacked after a long and tiring day.

3RD.—Started at 5 a.m. Marched to Rotterdam, arriving about 10 a.m. Some of the New Zealanders of Colonel Colville's Column went towards the Vaal, and were rushed by a party of Boers about 200 strong, losing one killed, two wounded, and 16 taken prisoners.

4TH.—Started at 5 a.m. with mounted troops and two days' supplies. Column marched to Waailwek. The squadron was sent to Spitz Kop to endeavour to open

JANUARY, 1902.

communication with Colonel Colville, and, after succeeding, returned to the column at noon.

The column off-saddled for an hour before proceeding to Onverwacht, on nearing which Valentine's Corps, which was in advance, was rushed by about 600 Boers. Valentine and 18 men were killed and 36 were wounded (three of whom died afterwards from wounds received), besides 36 prisoners being taken.

The Boers lost Commandant Opperman killed and nine men.

5TH.—Buried Valentine and other dead at 5 a.m., and the squadron marched at 7 a.m. as rear guard, with guns, to convoy, reaching the camp at Rotterdam at 7 p.m.

6TH.—Could not move till 7.30 a.m. owing to thick fog. Made a long march, viâ Balmoral, Glenfillan, and Vos Kop, finally turning into the valley and camping at Grootfontein. Convoy reached camp at 8 p.m.

7TH.—Started at 5 a.m., acting as right flank guard. Guns shelled about 50 Boers in Stoffel Botha's Valley.

8TH.—Started at 6 a.m. and marched to Hurricane Hill, near Wakkerstroom.

22ND.—No move was made until to-day, when the column marched as far as Grootvlei and bivouacked.

23RD.—Started at 12.5 a.m. and marched all night in pouring rain to Vos Kop, where we arrived at 5 a.m. Remained there in thick fog and rain until 10 a.m., when we returned to Grootfontein.

25TH.—Started at 12.5 a.m. Marched to Diepdal, on north side of Stoffels Valley. By the time morning broke the valley was entirely surrounded by columns under command of the following:—Pulteney, Colvin, Vialls, Colville, and men from Castrals Nek, Wakkerstroom, and the blockhouses. The V.M.R. and some of Colville's Column went into the valley and routed out 39 Boers, who were shelled from all sides, and, being unable to get away, surrendered at the blockhouses.

27TH.—Lieut. Partridge returned with 28 remounts.

JANUARY, 1902.

31ST.—Started at 12.5 a.m. and marched all night. Arrived at Rotterdam at 8 a.m., and off-saddled owing to fog. About 9 a.m., when fog lifted, went into the valley and got about 170 head of cattle and some mules and ponies. A party of Boers seen trekking in the distance towards Bank Kop.

2ND FEBRUARY.—Started at 8.30 p.m., and marched all night as rear guard to mounted troops. Columns co-operating to-day. Colvin in advance, Vialls support, and Pulteney reserve.

3RD.—Arrived at Mooifontein at daybreak. Colvin took seven prisoners and 500 head of cattle. Saw about 200 Boers break back and go in the direction of Klipfontein. Some sniping. Went after a party of the enemy through Reit Spruit, Sterkspruit, Brakfontein, to Vermaakraal. Bivouacked at 8 p.m., after covering 60 miles during the day.

4TH.—Started at 5.30 a.m. and bivouacked at Pamielfontein at 6 p.m.

5TH.—Started at 5.30 a.m. Marched to Roodepoort and bivouacked.

8TH.—Started at 5.30 a.m. Acted as rear guard to convoy to Rolfontein.

10TH.—Started at 7.30 p.m., and marched westward all night, arriving at Welterreden, and captured Boers. Returned to camp after marching 55 miles.

12TH.—Marched at 7.45 p.m., and, continuing all night, arrived at Mabusa River at daybreak. Proceeded as far as Rotterdam, which was reached at 3 p.m., when we bivouacked.

14TH.—Started at 6.30 a.m. with three days' supplies on light wagons. Marched as rear guard to column to Vos Kop. Bivouacked at 6 p.m.

15TH.—Could not move till 9.30 a.m. owing to fog. Marched to Spitz Kop, and on from thence to Grootvlei. Bivouacked at 5.30 p.m.

FEBRUARY, 1902.

16TH.—Started at 6.30 a.m. Marched to Reit Spruit and bivouacked.

20TH.—The last four days were spent in camp awaiting convoy. Took out two parties and conducted small reconnaissances on the 17th and 18th. To-day, with 50 men of the squadron and 50 Q.I.B's., and one company of Scottish Rifles, I was sent in charge of wagons to Wakkerstroom. Arrived at Naauwpoort and bivouacked at 8.30 p.m.

21ST.—Started at 5.30 a.m., and reached Wakkerstroom at 9.30 a.m.

22ND.—Started at 2 p.m., and marched to a spot about two miles north of Hurricane Hill, where bivouacked.

23RD.—Started at 5.30 a.m., and reached camp at Reit Spruit, where column was, at 11.30 a.m. Left at 7.45 p.m. as advance guard to column, and marched all night, passing Balmoral and Belhesua, and reaching Rotterdam at daybreak. Proceeded later to Goedehoep and bivouacked.

25TH.—Very wet. Did not move till 9.30 a.m. Marched to Rolfontein and bivouacked.

27TH.—Started at 8 p.m. Reached Tweepoort at midnight.

28TH.—Continued the operations, acting in conjunction with other columns, and after marching about 50 miles. Bivouacked without seeing a Boer. Bivouacked at Kromdraai.

2ND MARCH.—Moved camp to Darling, about four miles from Standerton.

3RD.—Started at 5.30 p.m. and marched all night as rear guard. Crossed the Vaal at Roberts' Drift. Colonel Wing's Column with us (18th and 19th Hussars and South Australians) in advance.

4TH.—Arrived at Uitzoek at daybreak. Manœuvred about, shelled a few Boers, and finally dumped down on the south bank of the Vaal at 7.30 p.m., after covering 65 miles.

MARCH, 1902.

7TH.—Crossed the drift and bivouacked on the north side during the afternoon.

8TH.—Marched as rear guard to Standerton, arriving at noon.

10TH.—Moved camp to the railway line. Captain Mort and Lieutenants Hindley and Howard joined with 130 men.

14TH.—Lieutenant Curell joined with 70 men. Colonel Pulteney's Column broken up.

Extract from the Dublin "Mail," 1st March, 1905, published by kind permission of the Editor.

MEMORIAL IN ST. PATRICK'S CATHEDRAL, DUBLIN.

UNVEILED BY THE LORD LIEUTENANT.

"Yesterday afternoon an interesting ceremony took place in St. Patrick's Cathedral, the occasion being the unveiling by his Excellency the Lord-Lieutenant of the memorial which has been erected in the Cathedral in memory of the officers, non-commissioned officers, and men of the 8th King's Royal Irish Hussars who lost their lives in South Africa in the service of Sovereign and country during the campaign. The memorial takes the form of an artistically designed bronze tablet, the work of Mr. F. Mowbray Taubmann, sculptor, of London. The solemn function naturally attracted a good deal of attention, and a congregation of large dimensions thronged the interior of the National Cathedral. The central aisle was lined by members of the corps, who, with drawn swords, presented a very fine appearance in their handsome

SOUTH AFRICAN WAR

uniforms. In connection with the ceremony a detachment of forty non-commissioned officers and men of the 8th Hussars came specially from Aldershot, and were in command of Colonel Duff, C.B., while four trumpeters were also present.

"The following officers of the 8th Hussars were present:—Colonel Duff, C.B., commanding; Majors Thoyts, Deare, Mussenden, and Campbell, Captains Lambert, D.S.O., Jennings, Mort, Threlfall, and Van der Byl, Lieutenants Allen, Curell, Partridge, Malet, Hon. R. Ryder, Brutton, Clegg, Blakiston-Houston, Alexander, and Armitage.

"The following former officers of the regiment were also present:—Lieutenant-Colonel Clowes, C.B., Lieutenant-Colonel Fell, Major Henderson, Major Burns-Lindow, Captain Page, Captain Anderson, Lieutenant Sir R. Levinge, Bart.; etc.

"Major-General Mussenden, the Colonel of the regiment, was unavoidably prevented from being present owing to his absence abroad.

"The Lord-Lieutenant arrived shortly before four o'clock, accompanied by the Countess of Dudley, and attended by Major Deare, 8th Hussars, and Lord Hastings, 7th Hussars, A's.D.C. His Excellency was attended from the Castle to the Cathedral by an escort of the 6th Inniskilling Dragoons, and a guard of honour drawn from and consisting of one hundred of the 4th Battalion Royal Fusiliers was drawn up in the North Close, and received the Viceroy by presenting arms and the band playing the National Anthem. Their Excellencies were received on behalf of the Cathedral Board by Mr. Charles Leeper, Mr. R. R. Cherry, K.C., and Mr. J. H. Nunn, LL.D., Registrar to the Dean and Chapter. General Lord Grenfell, G.C.B., Commander of the Forces in Ireland, arrived from the Royal Hospital, attended by an escort of Dragoons, and Major-General Vetch and

Brigadier-General Rimington were also amongst the distinguished military gathering present.

"A procession was formed, and as it entered the Cathedral the Dead March from 'Saul' was played on the organ with impressive effect by Mr. Marchant, the Cathedral organist. The procession took the following order:—Beadle, choristers, gentlemen of choir, constable, clergy; Rev. S. F. H. Robinson, Treasurer's Vicar; Rev. J. D. Kidd, Chancellor's Vicar; Rev. D. F. R. Wilson, Succentor; Rev. C. P. Price, Dean's Vicar; Canon T. L. Scott, Canon J. Lockett Forde, Canon R. G. M. Webster, Dean Tottenham, Canon White, Treasurer; Archdeacon Scott, Chancellor; Rev. H. J. Lawlor, D.D., Precentor, succeeded by the officers of the 8th King's Royal Irish Hussars; the Dean's Verger, the Very Rev. the Dean, D.D.; with his Excellency the Lord-Lieutenant, his Excellency's Staff, the Commander of the Forces, with his Staff. A shortened form of Evensong suitable to the occasion was used, the prayers being intoned by the Rev. D. F. R. Wilson and the Rev. J. D. Kidd. After the opening prayers the 'De Profundis' was chanted and the Lesson, taken from Rev. xix., 11 to 16, was read by the Dean's Vicar, and was followed by the Nunc Dimittis, sung to Harwood's setting in A flat. The anthem, 'Be thou faithful unto death' (Mendelssohn), was then rendered by the Cathedral choir with beautiful effect, the solo part being finely undertaken by Mr. Melfort D'Alton.

"The service having arrived at this stage, the special ceremony of the day was reached. The procession re-forming moved to the south aisle, where the monument is placed. The memorial was hidden from view by a large Union Jack, in front of which a low platform, covered with red baize, had been erected. The Succentor having said prayer, Colonel Duff, Commanding the 8th Hussars, requested his Excellency to unveil the memorial. The Lord-Lieutenant then formally performed the ceremony, using the words: 'I now unveil this monument, in the

SOUTH AFRICAN WAR

name of the Father, and of the Son, and of the Holy Ghost.' As the folds of the flag fell those in the immediate vicinity were enabled to view the handsome memorial. It bears the following inscription:—

IN MEMORY
of the
OFFICERS, NON-COMMISSIONED OFFICERS, & MEN
of the
8TH KING'S ROYAL IRISH HUSSARS
Who were killed in action or who died of wounds or disease during the
SOUTH AFRICAN CAMPAIGN, 1900-1902.

Lieutenant-Colonel P. W. J. Le Gallais.
Lieutenant and Adjutant P. A. T. Jones.
Lieutenant F. H. Wylam.

Sergeant A. Fosdyke, Corporal J. Conroy, Lance-Corporal G. Hunter, Lance-Corporal J. Lusher, Lance-Corporal P. Marshall, Lance-Corporal F. Battrick.
Trumpeter W. Cruse.
Privates—J. Rivers, A. Seaward, R. Tudgay, C. Abear, A. Langston, J. Gill, G. Folbigg, S. Scott, J. Reardon, J. Brandford, G. Bullen, F. Bird, A. Tubby, F. Hatton, O. Griffiths, J. Dunn, J. Coles, G. Taylor, L. Over, W. Fawcett, F. Powell, F. Walker, G. Pitchford, J. Mason, W. Mann, J. M'Aulay, J. Cooper, J. Kirwan, H. M'Ilvenny, J. Brown, W. Brown, J. M'Cormack, F. Chubb, W. Thompson, J. Brunton, D. Noone, T. Dawson, J. Balls, G. Gadd, J. Laird, J. Sedgwick, F. Gavin, W. Fitzgerald, Shoeing-smith G. Harold.

This Monument is erected by their Comrades and by Officers who have served in the Regiment.

"The Dean, accepting the custody of the memorial, said—Your Excellency, it is my privilege to accept, on behalf of the Cathedral Chapter, the custody of this bronze, which you have been good enough to unveil, in memory of brave Irishmen who died in the service of their country. There is no blazon of honours upon the bronze, although there might be, for the King's Royal Irish Hussars have a long history behind them. Old enough and distinguished enough in the 18th century to be granted the motto: 'Pristinæ Virtutis Memores' ('Mindful of Ancient Valour'), in the 19th century they proved themselves mindful of it again and again. The story of the Light Brigade at Balaclava is a story which we are not likely to forget—which the world will not forget. And this long death-roll testifies that in the last great trial of our arms the 8th Hussars bore themselves once more as soldiers should—as Irish soldiers do. But there is no blazon of honour, no word of pride on the bronze. And that is right; for in the House of God—as in the sight of God, in Whose just and merciful keeping are these brave countrymen of ours—fame is a lesser thing than faithfulness. It is because these men were faithful that their comrades have come here to pay this last tribute of loyal affection. It is because they were faithful that we are thankful that their names should be preserved in this historic church, whose richest treasures are its memories of the good and the wise and the brave—that so in years to come our children's children may show this monument which speaks of love and duty, of grief and devotion, and of faithfulness unto death, which is the gate of life.

"The hymn, 'Fight the good fight,' was then sung, and as the closing amen died away the trumpeters sounded the 'Last Post,' after which the Benediction was pronounced, and the hymn 'Ten thousand times ten thousand' was sung as a recessional. After the service most of the congregation remained to inspect the memorial to a brave band of soldiers who fought and died for their Sovereign and country."

Extract from Dublin "Evening Mail," 1st March, 1905, published with the kind permission of the Editor.

"Yesterday his Excellency the Lord-Lieutenant formally unveiled a memorial in St. Patrick's Cathedral in honour of the officers, non-commissioned officers, and men of the 8th Royal Irish Hussars who during the South African campaign laid down their lives for their Sovereign and country. In the graceful and eloquent words in which the Dean accepted the custody of the memorial he gave a notable expression to the feelings which inspired the project of erecting it, and at the same time set forth in language that cannot be improved the feelings which its inclusion amongst the notable memorials of the National Cathedral must invoke. 'It is,' he said, 'because these men were faithful that their comrades have come here to pay this last tribute of loyal affection. It is because they were faithful that we are thankful that their names should be preserved in this historic church—whose richest treasures are its memories of the good and the wise and the brave—that so, in years to come, our children's children may show this monument, which speaks of love and duty, of grief and devotion, and of faithfulness unto death, which is the gate of life.' It is a fitting tribute to brave and loyal men; and though there is no blazon of honours on the bronze, the comrades of the fallen soldiers will, no doubt, cherish these words as at once a consolation and an encouragement worthily to maintain the glorious traditions of so famous a regiment.

" For they are, indeed, glorious traditions. Few regiments can point to a storied past more rich in valiant endeavour and honourable achievement. During the two centuries that have passed since King William III. commissioned Colonel Conyngham to raise a regiment of dragoons in Ireland the regiment so raised has served in many countries and in many campaigns, and has played a notable part in the great work of building up and defending the Empire. A little over two hundred years ago it fought its maiden engagement in the war of the Spanish Succession, and on that occasion it beat back a French force outnumbering it by four to one, though the victory was dearly bought with the life of the gallant Conyngham. Colonel Killigrew, who succeeded to the command, also lost his life while charging at the head of his men. At the battle of Almenara the Royal Irish Hussars captured a body of Spanish horse, and, tearing the belts from the enemy's shoulders, placed them, a strange though honourable adornment, on their own. The rough and impromptu adornment of the stricken field was formally confirmed by the Commander-in-Chief, and for many years the regiment wore their belts across their shoulders, and were known as the 'Cross-Belt Dragoons.' In the 'Forty-five' this gallant Irish regiment helped at the undoing of the Young Pretender; a generation later it saw sharp fighting in the Netherlands; and towards the end of the eighteenth century it was sent out to the Cape of Good Hope, to be transferred, a few years later, to India, where many of its most glorious records were achieved. The Royal Irish Hussars were in India so late as 1889, and when they returned home they did so as the first British regiment to complete three terms of service in India, in each of which they distinguished themselves on active service. But brilliant as their Indian service was—and for nearly a hundred years they have borne the acknowledgment of it in the word 'Hindostan' on their standard and appointments—it was in the Crimea that they achieved an unforgettable glory. So long as the memory of man retains its seat the story of the 'Charge of the Light Brigade' will pass from generation to generation; and in that famous exploit—the Royal Irish Hussars may well recall it with pride—their regiment played not the least distinguished rôle. After that glorious but deadly charge, the Royal Irish, attaching to themselves a stray body of the 17th Lancers (and thus cementing, in the hour of battle, a friendship between the two regiments that has ever since endured) rode through three squadrons of Russian Lancers, and, in the judgment of Kinglake, saved from extinction the remnant of the Light Brigade, 'all that was left of them, left of Six Hundred.' In the South African War the regiment did its share of the hard work, as the names on the memorial bronze sadly testify. A grateful country, remembering the long and intimate connection of the Royal Irish Hussars with the land whose military reputation they have so worthily upheld, pays its

SOUTH AFRICAN WAR

tribute of honour and respect to those who have fallen. To those who have happily survived, and are now serving in the regiment, it can offer no better compliment than to express its complete confidence that, should the need arise, officers and men of the Royal Irish Hussars will be not less willing than their lost comrades to do their duty, and will do it not less devotedly, ' Pristinæ Virtutis Memores.' "

www.ingramcontent.com/pod-product-compliance
Lightning Source LLC
Chambersburg PA
CBHW031146160426
43193CB00008B/266